KU-272-219

THE GREAT GLEN WAY

by Paddy Dillon

2 POLICE SQUARE, MILNTHORPE, CUMBRIA LA7 7PY
www.cicerone.co.uk

© Paddy Dillon 2016
Second edition 2016
ISBN: 978 1 85284 801 9
First edition 2007
ISBN: 978 1 85284 503 2

Printed in China on behalf of Latitude Press Ltd
A catalogue record for this book is available from the British Library.

1:100K route mapping by Lovell Johns www.lovelljohns.com.
© Crown copyright 2016 OS PU100012932.
NASA relief data courtesy of ESRI

The 1:25K map booklet contains Ordnance Survey data
© Crown copyright 2015 OS PU100012932.

All photographs are by the author unless otherwise stated.

Updates to this Guide

While every effort is made by our authors to ensure the accuracy of guidebooks as they go to print, changes can occur during the lifetime of an edition. Any updates that we know of for this guide will be on the Cicerone website (www.cicerone.co.uk/801/updates), so please check before planning your trip. We also advise that you check information about such things as transport, accommodation and shops locally. Even rights of way can be altered over time.

If you find accommodation listed here that is closed or unwelcoming to walkers, or know of suitable accommodation that we have left out, please let us know. Similarly, if you are an accommodation provider who would like adding to the list, or taking off the list, do get in touch. The most up-to-date version of Appendix B, based on reader feedback, can be downloaded from www.cicerone.co.uk/801/accommodation.

We are always grateful for information about any discrepancies between a guidebook and the facts on the ground, sent by email to info@cicerone.co.uk or by post to Cicerone, 2 Police Square, Milnthorpe LA7 7PY, United Kingdom.

Front cover: A view of Loch Ness from the rugged garden in front of Loch Ness Youth Hostel at Alltsigh (Stage 35, S–N; Stage 2, N–S)

CONTENTS

A whitewashed pepperpot lighthouse marks where the Caledonian Canal joins Loch Lochy near Gairlochy (Stage 1, S–N; Stage 6 N–S)

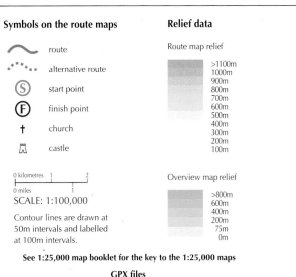

Symbols on the route maps

～	route
••••••	alternative route
Ⓢ	start point
Ⓕ	finish point
†	church
🏰	castle

```
0 kilometres   1          2
0 miles            1
```
SCALE: 1:100,000

Contour lines are drawn at 50m intervals and labelled at 100m intervals.

Relief data

Route map relief

>1100m
1000m
900m
800m
700m
600m
500m
400m
300m
200m
100m

Overview map relief

>800m
600m
400m
200m
75m
0m

See 1:25,000 map booklet for the key to the 1:25,000 maps

GPX files

GPX files for all routes can be downloaded for free at www.cicerone.co.uk/801/GPX.

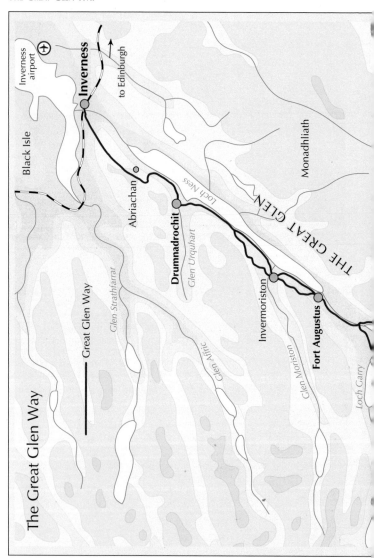

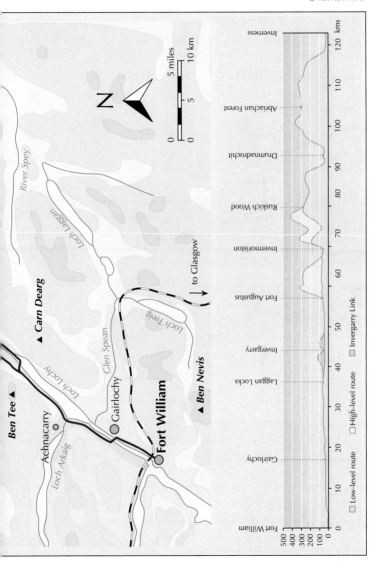

Legend: ☐ Low-level route ☐ High-level route ☐ Invergarry Link

Elevation profile stations: Fort William, Gairlochy, Laggan Locks, Invergarry, Fort Augustus, Invermoriston, Ruskich Wood, Drumnadrochit, Abriachan Forest, Inverness

Map labels: Ben Tee ▲, Achnacarry, Loch Arkaig, Loch Lochy, Carn Dearg ▲, Gairlochy, Glen Spean, Loch Treig, Fort William, Ben Nevis ▲, to Glasgow, River Spey, Loch Laggan

Scale: 0 – 5 miles, 0 – 5 – 10 km

N

The view from Inverness Castle, taking in the Cathedral and River Ness (Stage 6, S–N; Stage 1, N–S)

ROUTE SUMMARY TABLES

The Great Glen Way – south to north

Stage		Leg distance km (miles)	Ascent m (ft)	Page
1	Fort William to Gairlochy	17 (10½)	40 (130)	41
2	Gairlochy to Laggan Locks	19 (12)	330 (1080)	51
3	Laggan Locks to Fort Augustus	17.5 (10¾)	30 (100)	59
Invergarry Link		*+3.5 (2¼)*	*250 (820)*	*66*
2A	Gairlochy to Invergarry	26.5 (16½)	480 (1575)	66
3A	Invergarry to Fort Augustus	13.5 (8¼)	100 (330)	69
4A	Fort Augustus to Invermoriston (high-level)	12 (7½)	560 (1840)	71
4B	Fort Augustus to Invermoriston (low-level)	12 (7½)	300 (985)	77
5A	Invermoriston to Drumnadrochit (high-level)	22.5 (14)	710 (2330)	82
5B	Invermoriston to Drumnadrochit (low-level)	23.5 (14½)	600 (1970)	89
6	Drumnadrochit to Inverness	30.5 (19)	500 (1640)	97
Totals (low level without Invergarry Link)		**119.5 (74¼)**	**1800 (5904)**	

The Great Glen Way – north to south

Stage		Leg distance km (miles)	Ascent m (ft)	Page
1	Inverness to Drumnadrochit	30.5 (19)	540 (1770)	108
2A	Drumnadrochit to Invermoriston (high-level)	22.5 (14)	580 (1900)	119
2B	Drumnadrochit to Invermoriston (low-level)	23.5 (14½)	590 (1935)	126
3A	Invermoriston to Fort Augustus (high-level)	12 (7½)	710 (2330)	133
3B	Invermoriston to Fort Augustus (low-level)	12 (7½)	320 (1050)	139
4	Fort Augustus to Laggan Locks	17.5 (10¾)	40 (130)	145
5	Laggan Locks to Gairlochy	19 (12)	300 (985)	152
Invergarry Link		*+3.5 (2¼)*	*250 (820)*	*159*
4A	Fort Augustus to Invergarry	13.5 (8¼)	190 (625)	159
5A	Invergarry to Gairlochy	26.5 (16½)	400 (1310)	163
6	Gairlochy to Fort William	17 (10½)	10 (35)	167
Totals (low level without Invergarry Link)		**119.5 (74¼)**	**1800 (5904)**	

Great Glen Way Trek Planner

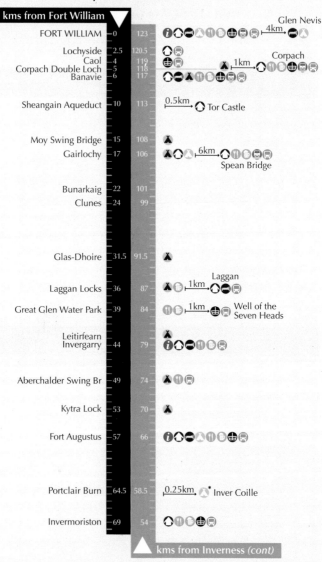

kms from Fort William

	kms from FW	kms from Inverness	
FORT WILLIAM	0	123	Glen Nevis 4km
Lochyside	2.5	120.5	
Caol	4	119	Corpach
Corpach Double Loch	5	118	1km
Banavie	6	117	
Sheangain Aqueduct	10	113	0.5km Tor Castle
Moy Swing Bridge	15	108	
Gairlochy	17	106	6km Spean Bridge
Bunarkaig	22	101	
Clunes	24	99	
Glas-Dhoire	31.5	91.5	
Laggan Locks	36	87	1km Laggan
Great Glen Water Park	39	84	1km Well of the Seven Heads
Leitirfearn Invergarry	44	79	
Aberchalder Swing Br	49	74	
Kytra Lock	53	70	
Fort Augustus	57	66	
Portclair Burn	64.5	58.5	0.25km *Inver Coille
Invermoriston	69	54	

kms from Inverness *(cont)*

12

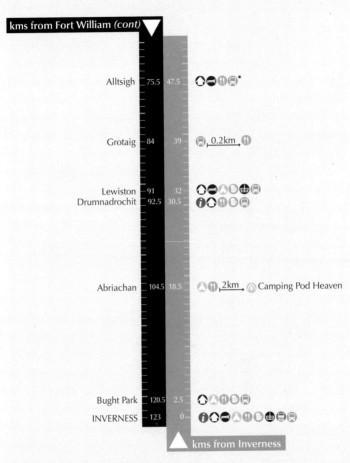

Alltsigh	75.5	47.5
Grotaig	84	39
Lewiston	91	32
Drumnadrochit	92.5	30.5
Abriachan	104.5	18.5
Bught Park	120.5	2.5
INVERNESS	123	0

Grotaig — 0.2km →

Abriachan — 2km → Camping Pod Heaven

kms from Inverness

ⓘ information centre ⚪ hotel/B&B ⬤ hostel/bunkhouse ⬠ camping pod
⬟ campsite with facilities ⚑ basic campsite ⬤ café/restaurant ⬤ pub/hotel bar
⬤ shop ⬤ train station ⬤ bus service ⟶4km⟶ distance off route

If not walking via the Invergarry Link, subtract 3.5km from the total distance.

If using the high-level route from Invermoriston to Drumnadrochit, subtract 1km from the distance.

Campsites marked ⚑ are very basic, either with no facilities at all, or with toilets requiring a key.

* Denotes facilities that are only accessible from the low-level route.

13

The path between the road and the shore of Loch Lochy, near Gairlochy (Stage 2, S–N; Stage 5, N–S)

INTRODUCTION

A view of Loch Lochy near Achnacarry, as a passing shower moves through the glen and leaves a rainbow (Stage 2, S–N; Stage 5, N–S)

The Great Glen is a remarkable geographic feature, running ruler-straight from coast to coast through the Scottish Highlands. Loch Ness, Loch Lochy and little Loch Oich are neatly arranged through the glen, while steep and forested slopes rise towards splendid mountains to north and south. Man has not missed the opportunity to run a road along this low-lying glen, and the Caledonian Canal was cut through the glen, linking its three lochs with the coast. Walkers are now blessed with the provision of a waymarked trail through the glen, running up to 124km (79 miles) from Fort William to Inverness via Invergarry and Fort Augustus. It was officially opened on 30 April 2002 by Prince Andrew, in his role as the Earl of Inverness. As a low-lying trail, most walkers could complete it at most times of the year, and there is always ready access to accommodation, food, drink and transport services.

The Great Glen Way provides an easy and scenic route through the Highlands, where walkers can admire the rugged mountains without having to climb them. Although much of the route can be covered by mountain bike, some paths are only for walkers. Take the time to delve into the long and turbulent history of clan rivalry, strife and warfare. Marvel at the engineering associated with military roads, railway lines and the Caledonian Canal. Keep an eye peeled for a glimpse of the celebrated Loch Ness Monster!

PLANNING YOUR TRIP

The attractive lock-keeper's cottage at Cullochy Lock near Aberchalder (Stage 3, S–N; Stage 4, N–S)

CHOOSING AN ITINERARY

The Great Glen Way can easily be walked within a week, and most walkers will aim to complete the route in five or six days. The daily stages are likely to be uneven, and while some will happily walk an occasional long day, others may prefer to split a long stage into two shorter days.

The first thing to decide is whether to walk from Fort William to Inverness (south to north), or Inverness to Fort William (north to south). From a practical point of view, walking from Fort William to Inverness means that you are more likely to have the sun behind you, with the prevailing wind, and hence the weather, at your back. Rainfall also tends to decrease markedly the further you go in this direction. However, the route becomes progressively more difficult, with the higher and more remote stretches coming towards the end.

Those who choose to walk from Inverness to Fort William can cover the hilly parts first, but should bear in mind that if bad weather is coming from the south-west, as it usually does, then they may be walking directly into it. The route does become easier and lower on the way towards Fort William, but the weather may become progressively wetter. Many walkers who have covered the route both ways are convinced that the scenery is better when walking north to south, or at least, they are more aware of it.

This guidebook describes the Great Glen Way in both directions; and given the connection with the West Highland Way at Fort William, there is no reason why both trails shouldn't be walked together in one long journey between Glasgow and Inverness, or vice versa. Many walkers also find themselves drawn to climb Ben Nevis while based at Fort William.

Most walkers will choose to trek through the Great Glen in the peak summer period. This can be a splendid time, weather-wise, with as much as 18 hours of good daylight. However, it is also a busy time and there can be a lot of pressure on accommodation and services along the way. The advantage is that all services will certainly be in full swing and are there to be used. Those who walk in spring or early summer will be able to enjoy the added colour of wild flowers along the way, while those walking in late summer should be able to catch the purple heather at its blooming best.

Summer is also the peak breeding season for the voracious 'midge'; a tiny insect (*Culicoides impunctatus*) that can cause distressingly itchy bites. Midges favour still conditions in the mornings and evenings, and are unlikely to be a problem in the middle of sunny, windy or rainy days. Most walkers move at a pace that outwits the midge, denying it a chance to land on the skin, but at every resting point, they seize the opportunity to feed on your blood. There are a number of repellants on the market, which meet

Weather conditions can change rapidly, but the Great Glen Way is essentially a low-level walking route

with mixed reviews from users: basically the less skin that is exposed, the less skin will be bitten.

Autumn brings its own delights, as the days are often cool and ideal for walking, and most services are still operating, though under less pressure. As the deciduous trees and bracken-clad slopes turn russet and golden, the scenery can be breathtaking. However, the weather can be wet, windy and misty at times, and some parts of the route may become wet and muddy.

Winter walking is possible, since the low-lying Great Glen is often free of snow even when there are deep drifts elsewhere. A thin covering of snow will not be a problem, but care should always be taken on icy slopes. Deep drifts, though short-lived, can make walking very difficult. Camping might not be the best option in the winter months, unless walkers are particularly hardy and possess the right gear for it. The chance to finish the day by a blazing fire in cosy lodgings has much more appeal, but bear in mind that not all the accommodation will be open throughout the winter months. Also note that midwinter daylight hours are very short: maybe as little as six hours!

TRAVEL TO THE GREAT GLEN

See Appendix A for the contact details of transport operators and information services.

Air

The nearest airport to the Great Glen is Inverness Airport (01667 462445, www.hial.co.uk/inverness-airport). There are direct flights to Inverness from major British airports such as London City, London Gatwick, Luton, Bristol, Birmingham, Manchester, Belfast and a few small Scottish airports. Most flights are operated by Flybe, www.flybe.com, and Easyjet, www.easyjet.com. Direct flights to Inverness from around Europe are available from Jersey, Dublin, Amsterdam, Geneva, Italy and Croatia. Stagecoach Jet Bus and local taxis operate from the airport into the centre of Inverness, which is very handy for the northern terminus of the Great Glen Way, or for onward bus services to Fort William. A much greater number of flights operate to Glasgow and Edinburgh, with most budget flights landing at Prestwick. All three airports have good public transport links to the cities for onward transport to the Great Glen by train or bus.

Rail

Cross Country Trains, www.crosscountrytrains.co.uk, Virgin Trains, www.virgintrains.co.uk and Virgin Trains East Coast, www.virgintrainseastcoast.com each operate long-distance rail services to Scotland. ScotRail, www.scotrail.co.uk, operates long-distance Caledonian Sleeper services into Scotland, and also provides onward rail services to Fort

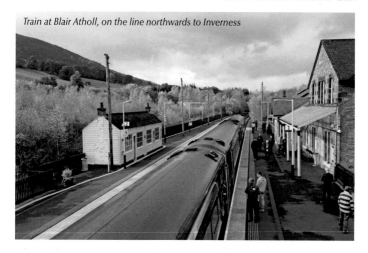

Train at Blair Atholl, on the line northwards to Inverness

William and Inverness. Walkers travelling from continental Europe can take advantage of combined Eurostar and Caledonian Sleeper services from Lille, Paris or Brussels in order to reach Fort William or Inverness refreshed and ready to start walking.

Coach

National Express coaches, www.nationalexpress.com, from all over England and Wales converge on Glasgow and Edinburgh to link with Scottish Citylink coaches, www.citylink.co.uk, to Fort William and Inverness. Walkers from around Europe can book coach travel through Eurolines, www.eurolines.com, that will include onward travel with National Express and Scottish Citylink coach services.

Car

Use the M6 and A74/M74 to travel north to Glasgow, then skirt the city on the M8 to follow the A82 north to Fort William. The A82 runs roughly parallel to the celebrated West Highland Way. Alternatively, use the A1 to reach Edinburgh and cross the Forth Road Bridge, then follow the M90 and A9 north to Inverness. Walkers who require safe parking for a week could have problems, but might be able to negotiate space with an accommodation provider.

TRAVEL THROUGH THE GREAT GLEN

Bus

Stagecoach Highlands, www.stagecoachbus.com, operates many services in and around the Great Glen. There are comprehensive town services around Fort William and Inverness, as well as a few buses through the Great Glen each day. Most of the buses through the Great Glen are operated by Scottish Citylink, www.citylink.co.uk. All bus services through the glen follow the main A82 road, serving Fort William, Spean Bridge, Laggan, Invergarry, Aberchalder, Fort Augustus, Invermoriston, Alltsigh, Drumnadrochit and Inverness. On average, buses operate every two hours, and the full journey through the Great Glen takes two hours.

With a careful study of current bus timetables, walkers could operate from a single base in the Great Glen, commuting to and from sections of the route each day. However, as the A82 is a busy road, drivers may insist that you use only the recognised bus stops, and they may not be able to stop at all on some parts of the road.

Car

The A82 is the main road through the Great Glen from Fort William to Inverness. Anyone accompanied by a back-up vehicle will find access to the Great Glen Way at several points, including Fort William, Inverlochy, Caol, Corpach, Banavie, Gairlochy, Bunarkaig, Clunes, Laggan, Invergarry, Aberchalder, Fort Augustus, Allt na Criche, Invermoriston, Alltsigh, Balbeg, Drumnadrochit, Abriachan Forest, Ladycairn, Blackfold and Inverness.

Cruises

The Caledonian Canal and the lochs it links create a coast-to-coast navigable waterway through the Highlands. Two barges – *Fingal* and *Ros Crana* – are operated by Caledonian Discovery (01397 772167, www.caledonian-discovery.co.uk), which sail back and forth between Banavie, near Fort William, and Inverness. These barges are equipped with berths for a dozen guests, offering unusual floating lodgings with a full meals service. Furthermore, passenger/guests may join week-long cruises and walk or cycle along parts of the Great Glen Way, returning to the barges further along the trail. It's also possible to paddle canoes alongside the barges. Alternatively, feel free to mix any possible combination of 'boot, bike or boat' through the Great Glen.

Shorter cruises are available on Loch Ness, where the Caledonian Canal runs into it from Fort Augustus. These are operated by Cruise Loch Ness (01320 366277, www.cruiselochness.com). The *Royal Scot* carries up to 120 passengers, has an on-board bar, and was designed to operate on Loch Ness. *Caledonian Spirit* is used for private hire, while two RIBs are also available, each carrying 12 passengers.

Traveline Scotland

Any public transport service, anywhere in Scotland, whether it is by bus, train or ferry, can be checked or confirmed simply by contacting Traveline Scotland (0871 200 2233, www.travelinescotland.com, or download their smartphone app).

Familiarisation with the Great Glen

Walkers can easily familiarise themselves with the Great Glen by driving along the main A82 road. The budget method of familiarisation simply involves catching a bus between Fort William and Inverness, watching the scenery passing by for two hours. For those with more time and money, travel at a more sedate pace through the Great Glen on one of the Caledonian Discovery cruises mentioned above.

FIRST/LAST NIGHT: FORT WILLIAM

While the Highlands and islands of Scotland can boast a long and proud Pictish and Gaelic history, the bustling town of Fort William is a relatively new development. There was little in the way of settlement up to the 17th century, until a wooden fort was built by General Monck in 1654, on the orders of Oliver Cromwell. A stone fort replaced it in 1690, built by General Mackay, who named it Fort William in honour of William of Orange. The town that grew alongside the fort was named Maryburgh. The Gaelic name for the town has always been An Ghearasdan, which means The Garrison. The Jacobites mounted a siege in 1746, but the fort stood fast.

Maryburgh was rebuilt with wood in 1750, so that it could be quickly burnt and destroyed in the event of a further siege, rather than fall into enemy hands.

Fort William prospered following the arrival of the West Highland Railway Company in 1889, allowing early tourists to reach the Highlands more easily. However, this led to most of the stone fort being destroyed. Most of the buildings seen around town are 19th and 20th century, and the West Highland Museum on Cameron Square is worth a visit (01397 702169, www.westhighlandmuseum.org.uk). The tourist information centre is at 15 High Street (01397 701801).

Facilities around Fort William include plenty of accommodation options, with a campsite and youth hostel available in nearby Glen Nevis. There are banks with ATMs, a post office, toilets, plenty of pubs, restaurants, cafés and take-aways. There are plenty of shops too, including several gift shops and outdoor equipment shops. Fort William proclaims itself the 'Outdoor Capital of the UK', www.outdoorcapital.co.uk. After a quick exploration of the town, most active visitors will be keen to head for the hills, or set off along walking routes such as the West Highland Way or Great Glen Way.

Fort William is served by good road and rail links, while town services are operated by Stagecoach Highlands (www.stagecoachbus.com).

LAST/FIRST NIGHT: INVERNESS

The origins of Inverness stretch back some 7000 years, and while Inverness Castle is basically an 18th-century edifice, it occupies a strategic site that has been fortified throughout the millennia. In AD565 St Columba visited the Pictish king Brude nearby. Shakespeare had Macbeth murder Duncan here in the 11th century, but the play is not a true record of history. Inverness was made a royal burgh in the 12th century and granted several charters, quickly establishing itself as a centre for trading and shipbuilding. The first bridge over the powerful River Ness was built in the 13th century, and a Dominican Friary was established.

Centuries of Highland strife saw Inverness suffer a succession of attacks and burnings, with peaceful interludes allowing for rebuilding, and its story throughout the Middle Ages was one of slow growth and increasing prosperity. When Cromwellian troops occupied Inverness in the middle of the 17th century, they built a garrison, of which only one tower survives. Jacobites occupied the castle in 1746, leaving it in ruins. Following the Rebellion, a huge fortified barracks was constructed outside the town, known as Fort George. Inverness continued to expand, and wooden buildings with thatched roofs were gradually replaced by more substantial stone structures. The town developed a thriving port and

gained several splendid buildings and new industries. While bridges over the River Ness proliferated, the Kessock Bridge between the Moray and Beauly Firth dates only from 1982. In the year 2000, Inverness was granted city status to take it into the 21st century. The city proudly proclaims itself as the 'Capital of the Highlands'.

Facilities around Inverness include plenty of accommodation, including a campsite and youth hostel, both handy for the city centre. There are banks with ATMs, post offices, toilets, plenty of pubs, restaurants, cafés and take-aways. There are also shops of all types, including gift shops and outdoor equipment shops. The Inverness Museum and Art Gallery is on Castle Wynd, below the castle, and the Tourist Information Office is in the same building (01463 252401, www.visitscotland.com). Those who wish to embark on a town trail can obtain information here, as well as information about services and attractions throughout the city and surrounding area.

There are plenty of bus services around Inverness, as well as into the surrounding countryside and further afield. There are also rail services, as well as a nearby airport.

BAGGAGE TRANSFER

Walkers wanting their luggage transported between overnight stops should contact the following operators: Great

Lodge in a lodge at the Great Glen Water Park (Stage 3, S–N; Stage 4, N–S)

Glen Way Baggage Shuttle and Support (01456 450550 www.lochnesstravel. com); and Great Glen Baggage Transfer (01320 351322 www.greatglenway baggagetransfer.co.uk).

ACCOMMODATION

A comprehensive accommodation booklet, updated each year and free of charge, is available from the Great Glen Way Rangers or tourist information centres along the Great Glen Way or it can be downloaded from the Great Glen Way website (see Appendix B). It is packed with all sorts of other information about the current range of facilities along the route, and should be obtained and carefully consulted well in advance of setting off. This guidebook indicates where accommodation is available, but the Great Glen Way Accommodation and Services Guide gives you the full contact details.

It is essential to book accommodation well in advance if you plan to walk during the peak summer season, as lodgings are very sparse in some places. If an address is some distance off-route, it may be possible to arrange to be collected in the evening and dropped off the following morning, but ask about this when making a booking. Accommodation can be booked while on the move, either through tourist information centres along the way or through Visit Scotland by telephone or through their website, www.visitscotland.com. Other online accommodation search and booking sites could also be used.

Always remember that when you make a booking with an

An attractive canal-side cottage and mooring stage near Cullochy Lock (Stage 3 S–N; Stage 4 N–S)

accommodation provider, a contract exists between you. If you fail to show, then you could lose any deposit paid, or even the full amount if already paid. Also, failure to show could cause concern for your well-being, and the rescue services might be alerted unnecessarily. If you think you will not be able to take up accommodation you have booked, please contact the provider and tell them.

Camping

While there are no campsites actually on the course of the Great Glen Way, some can be reached by walking a short distance off-route. Campsites can be found at or near Glen Nevis, Gairlochy, Invergarry, Fort Augustus, Drumnadrochit, Abriachan Forest and Inverness. There are small, basic,

free campsites available for single-night use at Moy Bridge, Gairlochy, Laggan Locks, Aberchalder, Kytra and the Seaport Marina at Inverness. Not all of these sites provide toilets, and those that do require users to apply in advance for a key, either via the Great Glen Way website, or through the Caledonian Canal office. Wild camping is possible in many places, subject to the provisions of the Land Reform (Scotland) Act 2003. Those who choose to camp wild for an occasional night should do so discreetly, well away from habitations, and keep their pitches scrupulously clean.

Hostelling

There are three Scottish Youth Hostel Association (SYHA) (www.syha.org.uk)

properties along the course of the Great Glen Way, which are insufficient to cover the distance. Walkers who wish to use the hostels may have to consider using bus services to reach them from certain points along the way. The hostels are located at Glen Nevis, near Fort William; Loch Ness, at Alltsigh; and Inverness, in the city centre. Bunkhouse and independent hostel accommodation is available at Fort William, Corpach, Laggan, Invergarry, Fort Augustus and Inverness, which should help to fill some of the gaps in the chain of SYHA hostels.

Hotels and B&B

There are plenty of B&B establishments through the Great Glen, as well as hotels in some places, offering a higher degree of comfort and privacy, at a higher price. If evening meals or packed lunches are required, please tell your accommodation provider when making a booking, since these may be difficult to organise at short notice. Some providers, while unable to offer meals, may be willing to take walkers to nearby restaurants for a meal, but again, ask about this when booking.

FOOD AND DRINK

There are plenty of places offering food and drink along the course of the Great Glen Way, but they are very unevenly distributed. In places such as Fort William, Fort Augustus, Drumnadrochit and Inverness, there are plenty of shops, bars, restaurants, cafés and take-aways available. In places such as Invermoriston there are only a couple of restaurants, while around Laggan and Gairlochy the choice is even more limited, and when places are closed it might be necessary to catch a bus elsewhere if you are not carrying food. Shops and places offering food and drink are mentioned throughout this guidebook, and if there are lengthy stretches where nothing is mentioned, then assume that nothing

A tempting sign near Abriachan Forest (Stage 6, S–N; Stage 1, N–S)

is available and be sure to carry some kind of drink and snack with you to cover the distance.

Fort William	01397 701801
Invergarry	01809 501424
Fort Augustus	01320 366779
Drumnadrochit	01456 459086
Inverness	01463 252401

TOURIST INFORMATION CENTRES

There are a handful of tourist information centres along the Great Glen Way (see Appendix A). Contact them for details of local facilities, including transport and accommodation, food and drink, and the opening times, locations and charges for nearby attractions. Some will be able to book accommodation for you, or at least point you in the direction of lodgings, and many of them sell useful maps and background literature, as well as gifts and souvenirs.

In certain places, the facilities on offer are numerous!

MONEY

Most accommodation and food providers along the Great Glen Way deal only in cash, though some will take cheques or credit cards. There are a few ATMs along the way, at Fort William, Spean Bridge, Fort Augustus, Drumnadrochit and Inverness, but bear in mind that some of these may be inside shops and may not be available on a 24-hour basis. Those who have never visited Scotland before will find that banknotes are issued by the Bank of Scotland, Royal Bank of Scotland and Clydesdale Bank, and these are used alongside Bank of England notes, so your wallet may often contain quite a variety of banknotes. Study them carefully if you are unfamiliar with them. Scottish banknotes are legal tender throughout Britain, though the further you travel from Scotland, the more difficult it can be to spend them, though banks are always willing to change them.

WHAT TO TAKE

Unless you sort out baggage transfers along the route of the Great Glen Way you are likely to be carrying everything you need for a week's

An idyllic loch-shore pitch, but is it legal to camp in the wilds? Refer to the Scottish Outdoor Access Code to find out

walk, so it goes without saying that you will need to pack essential kit only. Bear in mind that surfaces are generally hard tarmac or gravel, so light, comfortable walking shoes may be better than boots, but use something that you know works for you. If staying indoors, a small pack need only contain your usual walking kit, plus a change of clothes. Naturally, waterproofs should be packed, along with sufficient food and drink each day, plus a basic first aid kit for minor cuts and grazes. Full mountain walking gear is not necessary as the trail is essentially low-level and easy underfoot. The high-level routes created in 2014 are more exposed, but feature firm and obvious paths.

If backpacking, it makes sense to pack lightweight and low bulk.

A lightweight tent and sleeping bag will be fine for low-level pitches, outside of the winter months. Some campsites have showers and toilets, but there are also basic 'Trailblazer Rest' sites where a key has to be obtained in advance for the toilets. There are also a couple of sites with no facilities at all. If cooking meals, then pots, pans, stove and fuel need to be carried, but it is possible to buy food at shops along the way, to save carrying too much. If camping wild, pitches must be left spotless, and if relying on water from streams either satisfy yourself that it is drinkable, or treat it before drinking.

PLANNING DAY BY DAY

Walkers find a dusting of snow on the forest track above Loch Ness (Stage 5B, S–N; Stage 2B, N–S)

USING THIS GUIDE

The route is described both from south to north (starting from Fort William) and north to south (starting from Inverness) in this guidebook. The Great Glen Way is split into six stages, with high- and low-level options given for two of these. An alternative route past the northern side of Loch Oich (via Invergarry) is also described.

For each stage start and finish points (with grid references), distance in miles and kilometres, and total ascent in feet and metres are given. A note of the terrain to be encountered is included, and the relevant maps listed. Places to grab a bite to eat along the way, and details of public transport options relevant to the stage, are also included.

ADDITIONAL MAPPING

The linear extracts reproduced throughout this guidebook, showing each stage of the route in overview, are extracted from 1:100,000 Ordnance Survey data and the map booklet included at the back contains the full route on 1:25,000 OS mapping.

If you wish to consult additional mapping, the Ordnance Survey covers the Great Glen Way on three Landranger maps at a scale of 1:50,000. The sheet numbers are 26, 34 and 41. Three Ordnance Survey Explorer maps also cover the route at a scale of 1:25,000, and the sheet numbers are 392, 400 and 416 (www.ordnance survey.co.uk).

Harvey Maps produce a specific detailed map of the Great Glen

Way at a scale of 1:40,000 (www. harveymaps.co.uk). The maps that are appropriate for each stage are listed at the start of the route description.

In addition, all these maps are available in digital formats that can be downloaded and used with GPS-enabled devices and a full set of GPX files, for each stage described in each direction, are also available to download from the Cicerone website once you have bought this guidebook at www.cicerone.co.uk/801/GPX.

Walkers on the low-level Great Glen Way do not need to be concerned with specific mountain forecasts: it is sufficient to check the ordinary local weather forecast every evening after the news. What you hear might influence your choice between high-level and low-level options.

Walkers will encounter easy terrain and splendid waymarking along the length of the Great Glen Way. However do not rely entirely on the markers, which can disappear for all sorts of reasons. If you have not seen one for a long time you may have left the route at some to point and will need to turn round and walk back until you regain the way-marked route.

The Land Reform (Scotland) Act 2003 has established a statutory right of access to land and inland waters for outdoor recreation. The *Scottish Outdoor Access Code* gives guidance on your responsibilities when exercising access rights. The Act sets out where and when access rights apply. The Code defines how access rights should be exercised. The *Scottish Outdoor Access Code* is available on leaflets that can be obtained from Scottish Natural Heritage, tourist information centres and local government offices, as well as on the website www.outdooraccess-scotland.com.

The Great Glen Way is a way-marked trail so there are no access issues along the route. If you explore around the route, then normal provisions of the Scottish Outdoor Access Code need to be followed. You have a right of responsible access, subject to the Code:

A new path has been created above Fort Augustus (Stage 4A, S–N; Stage 3A, N–S)

- Respect the interests of other people: be considerate, respect privacy and livelihoods, and the needs of those enjoying the outdoors.
- Care for the environment: look after the places you visit and enjoy. Care for wildlife and historic sites.
- Take responsibility for your own actions: the outdoors cannot be made risk-free for people exercising access rights; land managers should act with care for people's safety.

The responsibility of recreational countryside users is to:

- Take responsibility for your own actions: the outdoors is a great place to enjoy, but it is also a working environment and has many natural hazards. Make sure you are aware of these and act safely, follow any reasonable advice and respect the needs of other people enjoying or working in the outdoors.
- Respect people's privacy and peace of mind: privacy is important for everyone. Avoid causing alarm to people, especially at night, by keeping a reasonable distance from houses and gardens, or by using paths or tracks.
- Help land managers and others to work safely and effectively: keep a safe distance from any work and watch for signs that tell you dangerous activities are being carried out, such as tree felling or construction. Do not hinder land management operations and follow advice from land managers. Respect requests for reasonable limitations on when and where you can go.

- Care for the environment: follow any reasonable advice or information, take your litter home, treat places with care and leave them as you find them. Don't recklessly disturb or damage wildlife or historic places.

- Keep your dog under proper control: it is very important that it does not worry livestock or alarm others. Don't let it into fields with calves and lambs, and keep it on a short lead when in a field with other animals. Do not allow it to disturb nesting birds. Remove and carefully dispose of dog dirt.

- Take extra care if you are organising an event or running a business and ask the landowner's advice. Check the full version of the Code for further details about your responsibilities.

RESCUE SERVICES

The Great Glen Way is essentially a low-level route and is usually close to roads and habitations, so there are few dangers. Obviously, common sense dictates that walkers should take care next to canals, rivers and lochs, as well as when crossing or following roads. The waymarking system is good, so route-finding difficulties are unlikely. If a marker has not been seen for some time, you may be off-route and it might be a good idea to retrace your steps. If the emergency services are needed at any point, police, ambulance, fire, mountain rescue and coastguard are all alerted by dialling 999 (or the European emergency number of 112). Be ready to give full details of the emergency, and give your phone number so that the emergency services can keep in touch. Members of the public cannot request direct helicopter assistance; their call-out and use will be determined by the emergency services based on the information you provide. A small first-aid kit should be carried to deal with any minor cuts, grazes and injuries along the way. Aim to be self-sufficient for each day by carrying food and drink in your pack.

GREAT GLEN WAY RANGERS

Should any problems be noticed along the course of the Great Glen Way, there is a team of rangers ready to address them. Contact the Great Glen Way Rangers, Auchterawe, Fort Augustus, Inverness-shire, PH32 4BT, 01320 366633. The official Great Glen Way website is www.outdoorhighlands.co.uk/long-distance-trails/great-glen-way-2. The former (and easier to copy) address www.greatglenway.com still redirects to the above address.

PHONES AND WI-FI

Mobile coverage is, as is usual in mountainous areas, patchy in places. When sorting out overnight stops in advance check with the accommodation provider about the provision of wi-fi and mobile coverage.

ALL ABOUT THE GREAT GLEN

A clear track follows the Caledonian Canal from Aberchalder to Kytra Lock (Stage 3, S–N; Stage 4, N–S)

GEOLOGY

If the Great Glen has a fault, then it is the Great Glen Fault! Even a casual glance at a map of Scotland reveals the true scale and extent of the Great Glen; a suspiciously ruler-straight trench running north-east to south-west. The underlying cause is geological, as the Great Glen lies on a major fault line. The fault has an incredibly long history, having become active some 400 million years ago. However, the rocks either side of it are considerably older. The fault is termed a 'strike-slip fault' and the land on either side has been displaced over a staggering 105km

(65 miles) or more. It is an interesting exercise to trace out a map of Scotland, cut with scissors along the Great Glen, then slide the northern half of the map that distance along the line of the fault. All other geological events being equal, that is what Scotland would look like if the Great Glen Fault had never existed!

Geologists have studied the granite bedrock near the villages of Foyers and Strontian, and although there is some dispute, many have concluded that they are essentially the same. However, these ancient granite emplacements lie on opposite sides of the Great Glen far distant from each other, ripped apart by the Great Glen Fault. The line of the fault is still considered active and it can give an occasional slight judder. Minor shock waves have been known to disturb the surfaces of the lochs, and structural damage has been caused in the past in Inverness. Earthquakes include one in 1816 that was felt throughout Scotland, with other notable events recorded in 1888, 1890 and 1901.

The power unleashed during such incredible movements has crushed an enormous band of rock along both sides of the fault, in places up to 1.5km (1 mile) broad. During the Ice Ages, when huge glaciers formed in the Highlands, the already weakened line of the Great Glen Fault was deepened considerably by the inexorable power of slowly moving glaciers. The broken rock along the line of the fault was more easily ground, crushed and moved than the solid rock of the mountains alongside, so that the Great Glen was carved considerably deeper than other Highland glens. As a result, low-lying hollows flooded when the ice melted, some 10,000 years ago, and have remained so ever since. The highest part of the Great Glen is occupied by the relatively shallow Loch Oich, while heading south-west Loch Lochy is broader and deeper. Heading north-east, Loch Ness is broader and deeper again, with its lowest parts being around 180m (600ft) below sea level!

Little Loch Oich sits at the highest part of the Glen and was flooded 10,000 years ago (Stage 3, S–N; Stage 4, N–S)

The Commando Memorial occupies a splendid site between Gairlochy and Spean Bridge, with rugged mountains leading the eye to Ben Nevis

ANIMALS AND PLANTS

The Great Glen Way starts and finishes on tidal inlets, and often runs within sight of broad lochs, stretches of canals and rivers. However, the glen is flanked by steep and rugged slopes, well forested for the most part, although there is some farmland on the floor of the glen. As there are a variety of wildlife habitats, there is plenty for an observant walker to see along the way.

The largest wild mammals are of course red deer, though there are also smaller sika deer and hybrids of both species. Deer are generally stalked from mid-August to mid-October, and anyone leaving the course of the Great Glen Way and heading for more remote places should be aware of this. The best places to observe deer are around the margins of woodland and forest at dawn and dusk, though they can be seen anywhere throughout the day. During the autumn, or 'rutting' season, red deer stags emit a deep-throated call known as 'belling', while sika deer make more of a whistling sound. The woodlands and forests of the Great Glen are strongholds of the red squirrel and pine marten, both in serious decline in many parts of Britain.

Scotland's native woodlands have been decimated over the past couple of thousand years. The most notable tree is the Scots pine, which is Britain's only native pine, and once formed extensive Caledonian forests. The Forestry Commission is playing a leading part in re-establishing this species. When growing close together, Scots pines form tall and straight trunks, with branches that die off, leaving a green crown. In isolation, the lower limbs of a Scots pine will often grow almost as thick as the main trunk, and are often bent into grotesque forms. Oak, birch, hazel, ash and rowan will be seen from time to time, but with so much land planted with imported conifers, deciduous woodlands are of limited extent. Beech trees flourish in many places, though these were introduced to the Great Glen.

While seabirds will doubtless be noticed at either end of the Great Glen, they are also found at many points along the way, using the low-lying, loch-filled corridor as they cross from coast to coast. Gulls, geese, ducks and even cormorants or shearwaters could be spotted at any point where they are attracted by water.

Also look out for grey herons as they patiently wait for fish, or more rarely, ospreys as they dive dramatically for a catch. Other birds of prey include golden eagles, buzzards, kestrels and merlins, while owls are also present. All seek small mammals such as mice and voles. Speak to a fisherman if you want to know what is in the lochs and waterways, or look out for salmon as they work their way inland to spawn late in the summer.

The growing season at such northerly latitudes is short, but summer days are very long and the abundance of water is an advantage for many species. While flowering plants may start to bloom late, they can continue to bloom long after the same species further south have set seed and died back. Few things compare with the sight of rampant flowery watersides in

Heron fishing on the River Ness near Inverness

early summer, or the purple heather on moorland slopes later in the season. Ling heather is dominant, but there is plenty of bell heather too. While red grouse can be spotted on heather moorlands, the rarer black grouse is most likely to be spotted on the Dochfour Estate near Inverness. In the autumn months, when the deciduous trees turn russet and gold, the scenery through the Great Glen can be astonishingly colourful.

THE LOCH NESS MONSTER

The year was AD565 and a follower of St Columba was swimming across Loch Ness to get a boat for his master. Suddenly, 'with a great roar and open mouth', a monster rose from the loch and bore down on the swimmer. St Columba swiftly intervened, commanding the monster, 'think not to go further, nor touch thou that man'. The monster sank back into the loch and caused barely a ripple of concern throughout succeeding centuries.

The whole world has seen the grainy black-and-white image that seems to show a tapering neck and head above the waters of Loch Ness. It is generally referred to as the 'surgeon's photograph' and was taken by the Harley Street consultant RK Wilson in 1934. Since that time there have been several 'sightings' of 'Nessie', as well as a number of amateur and professional 'hunts' around and within Loch Ness. Some photographs are easily dismissed as fakes, while others have enjoyed a period of notoriety before an admission of foul play is made. Vast sums

Some people believe the Loch Ness 'monster' to be an ancient plesiosaur, marooned in the deep water

of money have been sunk into the dark and murky depths of the loch, and while some might say that there has been little return for the investment, it has been great for tourism. One only needs to observe the coaches rumbling alongside the loch, or the cruisers that take trippers out onto the water, to say nothing of those who eagerly scan the surface for sight of something... anything. One man, Steve Feltham, has spent the past 24 years in a caravan beside the loch keeping vigil for Nessie, but announced his considered decision in July 2015 that the monster is probably a Wels catfish, introduced to the loch by Victorians for sport, rather than prehistoric.

There may or may not be a Loch Ness Monster, and in the absence of evidence one way or the other, visitors are free to believe what they wish. Two things are true: first, 'Nessie' does draw a lot of visitors to the area. Second, human beings have a proven capacity to believe almost anything, no matter how bizarre, and scientific proof is not always necessary. Those who are wavering in their belief are amply catered for at Drumnadrochit, where Nessieland and the Loch Ness Exhibition Centre clamour for attention. Shops throughout the Great Glen sell a variety of 'monsters', some smooth and sinuous, others plump and furry, some ferocious, but most of them happy and smiling, wearing kilts or playing bagpipes. You pay your money and you make your choice!

HISTORY

The history of the Scottish Highlands often seems remote from the history of the Lowlands. The Highlands were often inhabited by people with distinct cultural differences from those found further south. The Romans pushed into the area, but retreated. The Picts held sway for centuries, but were later eclipsed by the 'Scots', who came from Ireland. A thriving Gaelic civilisation existed in the Highlands throughout several centuries when Scottish history was wrought largely in terms of strife and warfare against England. Cromwellian troops subdued the Highlands in the 17th century, but there were notable rebellions in the 18th century, before the region was finally 'tamed'. The timeline history in Appendix C focuses on events in the Great Glen and the Highlands.

The Caledonian Canal

The low-lying Great Glen, with its three convenient lochs, was considered an ideal location for a coast-to-coast canal as early as 1726. However, Scotland was quickly embroiled in strife, and no further plans were considered until well after the Jacobite rising of 1745. Following a number of surveys, a serious proposal was put forward in 1802, and Thomas Telford was engaged to design and oversee construction. Although the Caledonian Canal is said to measure 96.5km (60 miles), only 35.5km (22 miles) is actually man-made. The cut sections of the canal were

A fishing trawler passes from Loch Oich towards Laggan Swing Bridge on its way through the Caledonian Canal (Stage 3, S–N; Stage 4, N–S)

engineered between 1803 and 1822; the first government-funded transport project in Britain. There are 4 aqueducts, 10 bridges and 29 locks.

The Caledonian Canal was created primarily to allow safe passage for naval vessels at the time of the Napoleonic Wars, but was not really used by the military until the Great War. As a through route for trading vessels, allowing a short cut through Scotland, the canal boosted the local economy. Large commercial craft still use the canal, but these days most vessels are leisure craft, plying through some of the most splendid canal-side scenery anywhere in the world. As the locks are operated by employees of British Waterways Scotland, they have set daily operating hours. Also, as there is a five-knot speed limit on the canal, even the most determined cruisers should allow a minimum of 14 hours sailing, spread over two-and-a-half days, to negotiate the Caledonian Canal.

Anyone interested in canoeing through the Great Glen should visit greatglencanoetrail.info, while those interested in cruising through should contact: Caledonian Canal Office, Seaport Marina, Muirtown Wharf, Inverness, IV3 5LE (01463 233140).

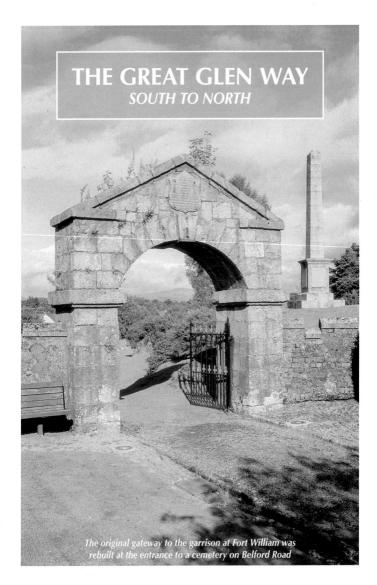

THE GREAT GLEN WAY
SOUTH TO NORTH

The original gateway to the garrison at Fort William was rebuilt at the entrance to a cemetery on Belford Road

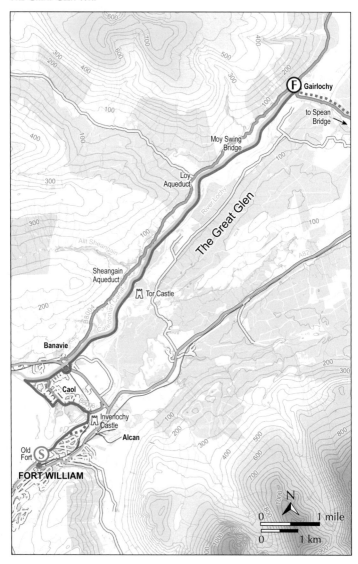

STAGE 1

Fort William to Gairlochy

Start	Railway station, Fort William (NN 105 742)
Finish	Gairlochy Bottom Lock (NN 176 842)
Distance	17km (10½ miles)
Total ascent	40m (130ft)
Time	4hr30min
Terrain	Low-level paths, tracks and roads near the coast, followed by a long, clear canal-side track.
Maps	OS Landranger 41, OS Explorers 392 and 400, Harvey Great Glen Way
Refreshments	Bars, restaurants, cafés and take-aways around Fort William. Shops and take-aways at Caol. Shops and bars at Corpach. Bar and restaurant at Banavie.
Public Transport	Stagecoach run most of the town bus services around Fort William, and also serve Caol, Corpach and Banavie. Trains between Fort William, Banavie, Caol and Corpach, as well as between Spean Bridge and Fort William. Shiel Buses run a limited schooldays-only bus service linking Fort William, Gairlochy and Spean Bridge.

The Great Glen Way starts near the coast in the busy Highland town of Fort William, in the shadow of Britain's highest mountain. This is an easy day's walk, largely along a canal-side track. There is very little climbing, and most of that comes in very short stages alongside canal locks. Most of the walk is on a long and narrow 'island', flanked on one side by the Caledonian Canal and on the other by the River Lochy.

Bear in mind that facilities decrease as the route unravels, and at the end of the day Gairlochy only offers a couple of B&Bs and a campsite off-route. During school term time there is a limited bus service linking Gairlochy with Spean Bridge and Fort William, but be sure to check the timetable carefully. Alternatively, ask in advance whether your accommodation provider is able to offer pick-ups and drop-offs.

For 1:25K route map see booklet pages 6–10.

Walkers starting at either the railway station or bus station in **Fort William** have immediate access to town centre facilities by way of an underpass. To find the start of the Great Glen Way, however, avoid the underpass and walk across Morrison's supermarket car park, then keep left of McDonald's restaurant. Note that the **Old Fort** is located on the far side of a busy roundabout, where a few low walls stand above the shore of Loch Linnhe. A stone monument marks the start of the Great Glen Way, and the route is marked throughout with signs bearing a 'thistle' logo. Note the design of the monument – two rock types joined at an angle, to mimic the Great Glen Fault.

> The original '**Old Fort**' was a timber structure built by General Monck to house 250 men. He referred to it as 'the fort of Inverlochy' in 1654, when writing to advise Oliver Cromwell of its completion. A stone fort was constructed in 1690 by General Mackay, housing a thousand men and defended by 15 guns. It was named in honour of King William, a member of the Dutch House of Orange, who fought a decisive battle against King James in that year. William ruled Britain jointly with his wife, Mary, the daughter of James II of Scotland. General Gordon attacked the fort during the 1715 rebellion, then in 1746 Sir Ewen Cameron attacked it. The fort was largely dismantled and the land bought by the West Highland Railway Company in 1889. They pushed a railway through the site, leaving only the small portion of the original walls seen today, which includes a sally port.

Leave the Old Fort and double back round the roundabout to find a tarmac pathway on the left side of McDonald's. This is signposted with the 'thistle' logo and soon passes a 'shinty' pitch (shinty is a popular Gaelic sport that resembles hockey). Briefly follow a brick-paved road past a few houses and cross a bridge over the River Nevis. Ben Nevis rises far inland to the right, while the waters of Loch Linnhe are a short distance downstream.

Turn left as signposted for the Great Glen Way and follow a gravel path that swings right, running roughly parallel to the tidal **River Lochy**. Alder trees tend to screen both the river and the Inverlochy suburbs of Fort William from sight. ▶ The path crosses a couple of small footbridges, then emerges from the wood into a rushy meadow. Go through a kissing gate and follow the riverside path past a sports pitch, then drift right to avoid using a narrow footbridge over the tailrace from the **Alcan** aluminium works. The flow of the water is so strong here that the little footbridge vibrates! Cross another bridge further upstream, then consider a detour beneath the railway line to visit **Inverlochy Castle**.

At peak high tides, there is an alternative route through the suburbs to the Alcan tailrace.

INVERLOCHY CASTLE

The Comyns were a powerful Scottish family with two branches, the Red Comyns and the Black Comyns. The Red Comyns built Inverlochy Castle (*Gaelic* – Inbhir Lòchaidh) in 1280 and surrounded it with a moat connected to the River Lochy. The four-square thick stone walls are protected by drum towers at each corner, the largest being Comyn's Tower. There was probably a timber-built Great Hall inside the walls. The castle is always open and there is no entrance charge.

The Red Comyns and Black Comyns supported John Balliol's claim to the Scottish throne, and therefore attracted the enmity of Robert the Bruce. The MacDonalds supported Bruce, and in 1297 their vessels engaged Comyn vessels off Inverlochy, resulting in the sinking of two ships. The Comyns were later defeated in battle at Inverurie in May 1308, and Bruce granted Inverlochy Castle to the MacDonalds. In the 15th century the MacDonalds were often in conflict with the Stuarts, who sat on the Scottish throne. Following a MacDonald raid on Inverness, James I sent a force commanded by the Earl of Mar to Inverlochy in 1431. As the army camped by the river they were picked off by MacDonald bowmen from the strategic hill of Tom na Faire, losing a thousand men. In 1645 there was another battle, this time between the Royalist army of Charles I, led by the Marquis of Montrose (with MacDonald support), and a Covenanting force led by the Marquis of Argyll (with Campbell support). Again, the strategic hill of Tom na Faire was put to good use by the Royalists; despite their smaller force they suffered only 20 casualties, while their opponents suffered 1500.

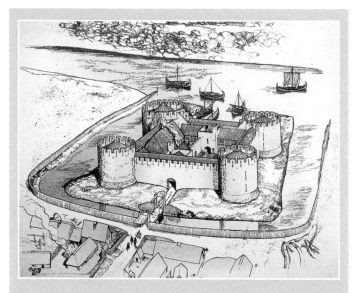

A plan of Inverlochy Castle, displayed beside the ruins, shows how it was originally surrounded by a moat

Following the construction of a fort at Fort William in the late 17th century (see above), Inverlochy Castle fell from favour. Military might was further consolidated when General Wade built a road from Fort William to Fort Augustus, passing Inverlochy Castle and completed in 1727. The castle was abandoned and was used by the Invergarry Ironworks from 1729 to 1736 as a store for pig iron.

Cross the Soldier's Bridge near Inverlochy Castle. This long wooden footbridge, mounted on top of a pipe, runs parallel to the railway bridge over the **River Lochy**. Walk up to the **B8006 road** and turn left to follow it down past a primary school and a B&B to reach the village of **Caol**. Turn left along Glenmallie Road, then turn right along Erracht Drive, which is flanked by a broad coastal green.

Caol (Gaelic – *Caol Loch Abar*) is a village close to The Narrows, where Loch Linnhe turns a right-angle corner and becomes known as Loch Eil. There are a couple of shops, pubs and take-aways, a post office, toilets and regular daily bus services to and from Fort William, Corpach and Banavie.

At the end of Erracht Drive continue walking along a gravel path hemmed in between the shore of Loch Linnhe and a sports pitch. Cross a footbridge and follow the path up onto the stout embankment of the **Caledonian Canal**. At this point, either turn right to follow the Great Glen Way onwards, or turn left to explore the nearby village of Corpach first.

CORPACH

Corpach (Gaelic – *A' Chorpaich*) is an interesting little village, well worth a visit, overlooking the western sea terminus of the Caledonian Canal. There is public access to the Corpach Sea Lock and Corpach Basin, where boats may be moored while they wait for a favourable tide. The Narrows nearby are dominated by a huge pulp and paper mill, which chews up trees from the surrounding forests. A popular attraction for those with an interest in geology is 'Treasures of the Earth', which focuses on mines, minerals, gemstones and fossils. Open daily, April to October 10am–5pm, July and August 9.30am–6pm. Limited opening in winter (01397 772283, www.treasuresoftheearth.co.uk). There is an entrance charge.

Corpach has a bunkhouse and a couple of independent hostels and B&B establishments. There is a post office inside the Co-op store, and an ATM outside. Toilets are available in the Kilmallie Hall, when open, while canal users have access to toilets and a basic camping pitch near the canal office. Another shop and a bar are also available, and there are regular daily bus and train services to and from neighbouring Banavie and Fort William.

Follow the course of the Caledonian Canal inland, climbing beside the Corpach Double Lock. A broad gravel track is followed, flanked on the left by grassy, flowery waterside banks, with fine trees on the right. Note the overspill weir, where excess water from the canal flows down into Loch Linnhe. The canal describes a broad and graceful curve to the left, with tall beech trees alongside, often obscuring views of Caol. Simply follow the canal-side track until directed by a marker post down a path on the right, not far from a little pub restaurant called Lochy. Walk along a road, over a level crossing near **Banavie Station**, and turn left to follow the busy A830 towards Banavie Swing Bridge.

Banavie (Gaelic – *Banbhaidh*) is a little village with only a few facilities, but take note of them as there is nothing else after this point. The Moorings Hotel, a couple of guest houses and a hostel are available, along with a canal-side gift shop that also offers teas. Basic camping is available beside the canal. There are regular daily bus and train services to and from Corpach and Fort William, as well as a schooldays-only service ahead to Gairlochy.

Cross the road without crossing the bridge, then climb uphill in stages beside the celebrated rise of locks known as Neptune's Staircase.

Neptune's Staircase is an inspired name for the tightly packed series of eight canal locks at Banavie. The arrangement is difficult to see in its entirety, and the best views are those seen in the aerial shots used for postcards. Canal cruisers can pass from top to bottom in about ninety minutes, including the road and rail swing bridges at the bottom, but the time taken can almost double if craft pass through in the other direction at the same time.

The upper part of Neptune's Staircase is Banavie Top Jetty. Follow the broad gravel canal-side track onwards, passing through a gate beside tall pines. The canal curves gently right and left and for brief periods there are no signs of habitation. A splendid variety of trees flank both banks. It is quite possible to cross the **Sheangain**

Aqueduct without noticing, but take a few minutes to have a proper look at it.

Use a narrow path to descend from the embankment to gain a view of the three arched tunnels. Two carry water from the **Allt Sheangain**, while the third covers a stone-paved passage for man and his animals.

Not far from the Sheangain Aqueduct, **Tor Castle** overlooks the River Lochy. It was built by the MacIntoshes, who vacated it towards the end of the 13th century. Some time later it was occupied by the Camerons, sparking a feud between the two clans that spanned some 350 years, continuing even after the Camerons abandoned the property in 1660 and went to settle in Achnacarry. There is a B&B near the castle.

Continue enjoying the variety of trees alongside, and look across the water to spot a stream feeding water into the canal. Pass a cottage where the track rises gently, then falls gently, passing abundant birch trees on the little hill of Druim na h-Atha. The track later crosses an overspill weir, where excess water flows down into the River Lochy. Look across the canal to see a knoll crowned with a few pine trees, which is an old burial ground. Further along, the canal crosses the **Loy Aqueduct**, built over the River Loy.

To see the **Loy Aqueduct** properly, you must drop down a track on the right well beforehand, then retrace your steps. It is a splendid structure; the River Loy flows through a large central arch, while smaller arches on either side allow passage for man and beast.

Continuing along the canal-side track, the trees diminish, allowing views across small meadows near the River Lochy. The attractive white **Moy Swing Bridge** comes into view.

The attractive Moy Swing Bridge is the only bridge on the Caledonian Canal that has to be operated manually

The **Moy Swing Bridge** simply allows the farmer from Moy to drive tractors and trailers down to his riverside meadows. Canal traffic, meanwhile, relies on a keeper to open and close the bridge on demand. However, the bridge is not mechanised, and only one half can be opened manually at a time; hence the need for a small boat so that the keeper can row across and open the other half. Basic camping, with no facilities, is permitted near the bridge.

Just beyond the bridge, look across the canal to spot another inflowing stream. Also, look out for another knoll with distinctive pine trees on the far bank, which is another old burial ground. Tall beech trees again grace the canal-side. Follow the track across an overspill weir and enjoy a fine view of the broad and shingly River Lochy. Looking back you can see Ben Nevis rising majestically from the Great Glen. Climb past Gairlochy Bottom Lock to reach a swing bridge on the narrow B8004 road at **Gairlochy**.

Walkers with time to spare can cross the road and continue along the canal-side track. A slight climb leads past Gairlochy Top Loch, where the canal broadens into a mooring basin. Continue beyond a gate and follow a grassy path along an embankment to reach a small white lighthouse where there is a fine view along the length of Loch Lochy. Steps must be retraced to the road afterwards.

GAIRLOCHY

Gairlochy (Gaelic – *Gèarr Lòchaidh*) is 6km (4 miles) has won, or come runner-up, in the 'Waterway Length Competition' on several occasions. Note that Gairlochy isn't a village, but merely a scattering of houses, and if anything can't be obtained in the locality, then it is necessary to move far off-route.

Basic camping is permitted near the canal, but a key for the toilet at the canal lock must be obtained in advance via the Great Glen Way website or Caledonian Canal office. The Dalcomera B&B is the only lodging nearby, just a short walk along the B8004 road. This road also leads to the Gairlochy Holiday Park, which has a serviced campsite. Any further facilities are well off-route at Spean Bridge. Shiel Buses run a very limited schooldays-only service linking Gairlochy with Spean Bridge and Fort William. The nearest taxi service operates from Fort William.

A boat on the Caledonian Canal between Gairlochy Top Lock and Gairlochy Bottom Lock

SPEAN BRIDGE

Spean Bridge (Gaelic – *Drochaid Aonachain*) is 6km (4 miles) away from Gairlochy. The High Bridge, built by General Wade in 1736, was the first bridge to span the rocky gorge beside the village. The West Highland Railway, built to serve Fort William from 1889, was equipped with a station at Spean Bridge. Outside the village, at a junction with the Gairlochy road, is the celebrated Commando Memorial, dating from 1952.

There are a few accommodation options around Spean Bridge, including a hotel. There is a post office shop, with an ATM outside, as well as a restaurant. Regular daily Scottish Citylink bus services run to and from Fort William, Fort Augustus and Inverness. Stagecoach Highland buses run to and from Fort William, while schooldays-only Shiel Buses link Spean Bridge with Fort William and Gairlochy. Trains run to Fort William and Glasgow. Some accommodation providers in Spean Bridge offer lifts to and from Gairlochy, if given due notice.

The Commando Memorial lies off-route, but can be visited by those who head to Spean Bridge for accommodation (Stage 1, S–N; Stage 6, N–S)

STAGE 2
Gairlochy to Laggan Locks

Start	Gairlochy Bottom Lock (NN 176 842)
Finish	Laggan Locks (NN 286 96)
Distance	19km (12 miles)
Total ascent	330m (1080ft)
Time	4hr 30min
Terrain	Clear, firm paths, minor roads, forest tracks and canal-side path.
Maps	OS Landranger 34, OS Explorer 400, Harvey Great Glen Way
Refreshments	The *Eagle* bar/restaurant at Laggan Locks.
Public Transport	Schooldays-only Shiel Buses linking Fort William, Gairlochy and Spean Bridge, which will divert to Achnacarry on request to the driver. Regular daily Scottish Citylink buses link Laggan with Fort William, Fort Augustus and Inverness.

This whole day's walk runs close to the northern shore of Loch Lochy. The slopes rising from the loch are often well wooded or forested, so that the water is only glimpsed from time to time. Timber harvesting and replanting in the forests ensure that, over time, views will change. Detours from the Great Glen Way can be considered around Achnacarry, either to see St Ciaran's Church, tucked away in the woods, or to visit the Clan Cameron Museum. This is essentially Cameron country (or at least it became so after the Camerons concluded a 350-year feud against the MacIntoshes!). The land around Achnacarry was once used as a training ground for commandos.

Bear in mind that once you leave Clunes there is no exit from the long, forested loch-side track until the end of the stage. Laggan Locks on the Caledonian Canal concludes the day's walk, where nearby facilities are very limited. Some walkers might prefer to follow the Invergarry Link instead (see Stages 2A and 3A).

For 1:25K route map see booklet pages 10–17.

Leave **Gairlochy** by crossing the swing bridge, then turn right to follow the **B8005**, which is signposted for Loch Arkaig. Keep straight ahead at a junction, then turn left as marked up a gravel path. This path undulates across a forested slope just above the road, then later drops down to cross it. A short, steep descent leads to the shore of **Loch Lochy**. Look back towards Gairlochy to spot a prominent little lighthouse and signs that indicate where the Caledonian Canal joins the loch.

The level of **Loch Lochy** was raised 3.65m (12ft) during the construction of the Caledonian Canal. Its surface level is now 28.5m (94ft) above sea level, and its maximum depth is 40.5m (133ft). The loch is just short of 16km (10 miles) in length and only exceeds 1.5km (1 mile) in width at one spot. It is said to be inhabited by a monster known as 'Lizzie', no doubt related to 'Nessie'.

A winter day on the shore of Loch Lochy near Bunarkaig

Follow the clear, firm gravel path along the shore, which features fine beech trees. Cross a footbridge and

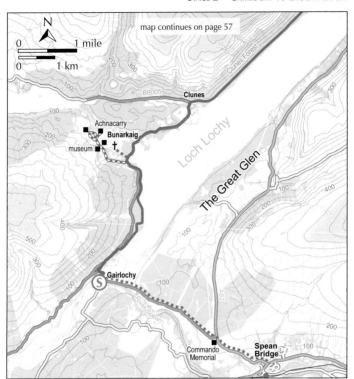

map continues on page 57

note how much moss thrives beneath the trees, covering boulders and fallen tree trunks in soft, bright green, rumpled velvet. Later, birch trees fringe the loch shore and densely packed conifers allow little light to reach the ground. The path drifts away from the shore. Cross a footbridge over the Allt Coire Choille-rais. Later, the shoreline path crosses two footbridges as it runs round a small bay, then climbs gradually across a slope of gnarled oaks, slender birch, beech and alder. Continue along the **B8005 road** to reach a cluster of houses, where a sign invites visitors to make a detour to the **Clan Cameron Museum** at Achnacarry.

CLAN CAMERON

The Clan Cameron has a long association with the Great Glen. Originally, there were three families: the McMartins of Letterfinlay, the McGillonies of Strone and the McSorlies of Glen Nevis. The first Chief of the combined families was Donald Dubh, born around 1400, and the most recent is Donald Angus Cameron of Locheil, the 27th Chief. Never shy of battle, the Camerons were described as 'fiercer than fierceness itself'. Their rallying cry was 'Sons of the hounds, come hither and get flesh!' The Camerons moved from Tor Castle to Achnacarry around 1660, and visitors will appreciate the attractions of the location, an easily defended mountain fastness with sheltered pasture.

The 19th Chief, the 'Gentle Locheil', supported Bonnie Prince Charlie in 1745, thus ensuring that many other clans rallied to the cause. Despite early military success, the Prince's forces were soundly beaten at Culloden and Charles was lucky to escape with his life. In retribution for Locheil's support, the Duke of Cumberland destroyed the original timber-built Achnacarry House in 1746, and Locheil fled into exile. The current stone-built house dates from 1802, and the Clan Cameron has distinguished itself by raising generations of soldiery for the Queen's Own Cameron Highlanders. Achnacarry House was occupied by the military for most of the Second World War, when it was the Commando Basic Training Centre, featuring one of the most gruelling military training regimes in the world.

A detail from one of the stained glass windows in St Ciaran's Church, just off-route near Achnacarry

If you are a Cameron – and that includes members of nearly seventy 'sept' or sub-branch families! – then you should feel obliged to make a detour to the **Clan Cameron Museum**. The Museum, housed in a whitewashed 17th-century croft, is open from April to early October, 1.30–4.30pm, but 11am–5pm in July and August. There should be a notice by the gates on the B8005 road if the museum is open. There is an entrance charge (01397 712480, **www.clancameronmuseum.co.uk** and **www. clan-cameron.org**).

Another short detour could be made to St Ciaran's Church, in a quiet woodland setting. Watch out for a sign showing the way along a track. Continue along the B8005 road, crossing a bridge over the River Arkaig at **Bunarkaig**.

Later, a fine variety of trees grace the landscape. The most striking conifers are the giant redwoods, or sequoias, while the most impressive deciduous trees are the copper beeches. The most colourful are undoubtedly the rhododendrons when in bloom, but they do have a habit of choking out other species over time. The land near Loch Lochy is very wet and boggy, supporting profuse growths of bog myrtle. Pass a large white house and modest forestry houses at **Clunes**, then turn right along a forest track. This passes a couple of houses and some wooden cabins, one of which is the Clunes Forest School. ▶

Occasionally, the Great Glen Way Rangers station themselves at the Forest School and welcome the opportunity to have a chat with walkers.

Go through a tall gate to leave a car park and follow the forest track parallel to the shore of Loch Lochy. The track undulates and passes commercial conifers, as well as self-seeded alder and birch scrub, along with bracken, brambles and tufts of heather. Pass a small waterfall and a gateway on the Allt na Molaich to walk through a more mature part of the forest. The track dips downhill, then climbs gently, passing another gateway before descending again. On the next gentle ascent and descent, clear-felling allows good views across the loch, then after crossing a bridge over the **Allt Glas-Dhoire Mór**, the track passes through another area of mature forest. There is a stretch at a lower level through younger forest, with a margin of alder scrub, where there are more views across the loch.

Pass a tall gateway and walk among tall trees, again with no views. Cross a bridge over the **Allt Glas-Dhoire** and drop steeply downhill a short way.Just off-route, beside the loch near the ruins of Glas-Dhoire, is a basic 'Trailblazer Rest' campsite. ▶ The track continues close to the shore of the loch and the trees are remarkably mixed, with conifers, alder and birch. When the track climbs markedly uphill, it is almost exclusively flanked by birch. A junction of tracks is reached near a communication mast, where a right turn is made. Go through a tall gate and continue straight ahead, passing the access for the Highland Lodges. Enjoy views over the head of Loch Lochy on the way downhill, then cross a bridge at **Kilfinnan Farm** to continue along a narrow tarmac road.

A key for the toilet needs to be obtained in advance via the Great Glen Way website or Caledonian Canal office.

When a junction is reached, the route keeps right and crosses a cattle grid, but note that the Invergarry Link heads left (see Stage 2A).

When the road enters a forest, turn right along another narrow road to pass some wooden lodges, and keep right along the flat to walk along a causeway road, crossing boggy ground beside Ceann Loch, to reach **Laggan Locks**. These are double locks, and the Caledonian Canal needs to be crossed at the lock gates. Once across, the route turns left, but it is also possible to leave the route and head straight for the main road, where there are bus stops. Facilities around **South Laggan** and North Laggan are sparse, and some walkers might like to walk a little further by using the Invergarry Link.

A winter view from Laggan Locks, across Ceann Loch, at the head of Loch Lochy

A conflict known as the **'Battle of the Shirts'** took place at Laggan in the 16th century. The seeds were sown, as was often the case among Highland

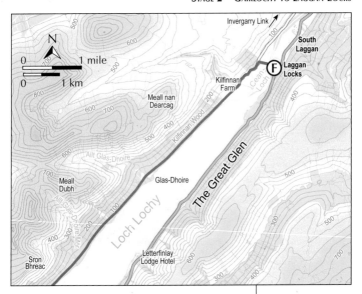

clans, with a perceived insult. Ranald Galda, of Clanranald, had been reared among the Frasers, and when he returned to his home a feast was prepared by way of welcome. As seven oxen were slaughtered, Ranald remarked that a few hens would have been sufficient, thus spurning the hospitality of his hosts. They called him 'Ranald of the Hens' and said that he could return to the Frasers if he didn't like it.

It was an uncomfortably hot day in 1544 when 300 Frasers faced a combined force of 600 MacDonalds and Camerons to settle the score. Both sides had to put aside their hot and heavy woollen plaids and fight each other wearing long undershirts; hence the name 'Battle of the Shirts'. Neither side scored a victory, since the carnage was so great that only four Frasers and eight of their opponents were left standing at the conclusion of the battle.

The 'Eagle' is also known as 'The Inn-on the Water', offering a floating bar and restaurant at South Laggan

LAGGAN

Laggan (Gaelic – *Lagan*) is a sprawling settlement with no clear centre. South Laggan is the area near Laggan Locks, while North Laggan is closer to the Laggan Swing Bridge, over 2km (1¼ miles) away. Facilities are limited to the Great Glen Hostel and a couple of B&B places. Basic camping is available near the locks. The *Eagle* is a converted Dutch barge that operates as a floating bar/restaurant near Laggan Locks; another restaurant can be found at the Great Glen Water Park on the shores of Loch Oich (see Stage 3). Regular daily Scottish Citylink buses link Laggan with Fort William, Fort Augustus and Inverness.

STAGE 3

Laggan Locks to Fort Augustus

Start	Laggan Locks (NN 286 963)
Finish	Tourist Information Centre, Fort Augustus (NH 378 094)
Distance	17.5km (10¾ miles)
Total ascent	30m (100ft)
Time	4hr 30min
Terrain	Tracks and paths beside Loch Oich can be wet and muddy. A clear and firm canal-side track leads onwards to Fort Augustus.
Maps	OS Landranger 34, OS Explorer 400, Harvey Great Glen Way
Refreshments	Restaurant and bar at the Great Glen Water Park. Tea garden at Aberchalder Swing Bridge. Plenty of restaurants, cafés, take-aways and bars around Fort Augustus.
Public Transport	Regular daily Scottish Citylink buses link Laggan and Fort Augustus with Fort William and Inverness.

This is a splendid day's walk, starting with an easy stroll alongside the Caledonian Canal. The walls of the Great Glen rise closer to hand and there are often views of high mountains beyond. The Great Glen Way leaves North Laggan and continues along the southern shore of Loch Oich, where the richly wooded slopes are protected as a nature reserve. The course of an old railway line, as well as a stretch of General Wade's military road, are followed along the shore. At Aberchalder, there is an opportunity to admire the cunningly designed Bridge of Oich. Another lovely stretch of the Caledonian Canal leads onwards, gradually locking down until a steep flight of five locks drops down through Fort Augustus into Loch Ness. As this is a relatively short and easy stage, some walkers choose to pass straight through the bustling village of Fort Augustus and continue along the Great Glen Way to Invermoriston.

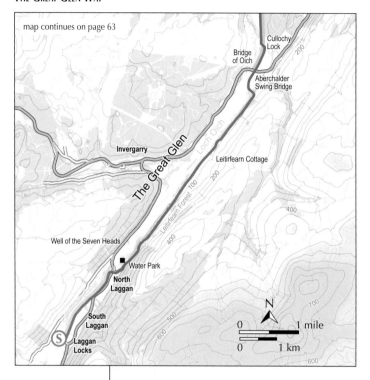

map continues on page 63

Cullochy Lock

Bridge of Oich

Aberchalder Swing Bridge

Loch Oich

Invergarry

The Great Glen

Leitirfearn Cottage

Leitirfearn Forest 100 200

400

400

Well of the Seven Heads

Water Park

North Laggan

South Laggan

(S) Laggan Locks

N

0   1 mile

0   1 km

For 1:25K route map see booklet pages 17–22.

Leave **Laggan Locks** by following a grassy track along the top of the canal-side embankment, passing the *Eagle* barge and bar/restaurant. The track reaches a slope of pine trees and dwindles to a narrow gravel path. The tree cover becomes more varied, with rhododendron and broom becoming common. All of a sudden, there is access on the right to the A82 road, not far from the Great Glen Hostel in **South Laggan**. Take care if following the road there, as it can be very busy.

Continue along the path by crossing a footbridge over a canal feeder, the Allt an Lagain. There is later a good view along the canal, from high above a mooring stage, where broom, gorse and brambles grow. Follow the path through an area of bracken to reach the A82 road again, near the Laggan Swing Bridge. ▸

A sign points off-route for the Well of the Seven Heads store. The shop is over 1km (½ mile) away and the road to it can be very busy.

Loch Oich is the smallest of the three lochs linked by the Caledonian Canal. It measures 6.5km (4 miles) in length and is only 0.5km (0.3 miles) across at its widest point. Loch Oich's greatest depth is 40.5m (133ft), but it had to be deepened at both ends to accommodate traffic using the Caledonian Canal. The surface level of the loch is 32m (105ft), which is also the summit level for the canal.

Cross the main road to follow a quiet road into the **Great Glen Water Park**, on the shores of **Loch Oich**, where there is a bar and restaurant surrounded by wooden holiday chalets. There is no need to follow the access road as directed to reach the bar and restaurant; simply stay on the road marked as the Great Glen Way and the building is quite close to hand just as the route leaves the road.

The path alongside Loch Oich often runs across a well-wooded slope

The **Invergarry and Fort Augustus Railway Museum** (www.invergarrystation.org.uk) is being developed adjacent to the water park. A section of railway track has been restored.

Head right up a track into woods where there are clumps of rhododendron. The track becomes aligned to an old railway trackbed, which features some cuttings. The surroundings are vividly green and are managed as a nature reserve. Step down from the trackbed later and go through a gate to follow the course of an old military road along the shore of Loch Oich. Keep dogs under control as sheep graze around here.

Leitirfearn Forest Nature Reserve features a lush, damp, vibrantly green woodland: a mix of ash, birch, elm and hazel. The steep slopes support cushions of moss and delicate ferns, as well as flowers in spring and fungi in autumn. It has the appearance of a jungle, yet it has been cut back twice to accommodate a road and railway. General Wade pushed a road through the woods around 1725, while the Invergarry and Fort Augustus Railway Company opened a line here in 1903. Both routes fell from favour, the road switching to the other side of the loch and the railway being abandoned in 1946.

There are views across the loch from time to time when the trees thin out, and the ruins of Invergarry Castle might be seen on the far shore. Watch out for a crenellated concrete arch on the right, which supports the former railway trackbed. Pass the old whitewashed **Leitirfearn Cottage** and follow a grassy track through a small meadow. ◄ The track runs through woods and briefly touches the shore again, before rising steeply to avoid a cliff. Climb through a rocky, mossy cutting, crossing over an old railway tunnel. When the track runs gently downhill, watch out for a miniature iron aqueduct on the left, carrying water across the old line. Cross a bridge at a small waterfall and reach a couple of gates.

A basic 'Trailblazer Rest' campsite is available. A key for the toilet needs to be obtained in advance via the Great Glen Way website or Caledonian Canal office.

Ahead lies the Aberchalder Estate Road. The Great Glen Way, however, turns left at the gates, then crosses an old railway bridge over the Calder Burn. Turn left at a kissing gate to follow a path beside **Loch Oich**, then cross a ladder stile and continue along a canal-side path to reach the **Aberchalder Swing Bridge** (from where the **Bridge of Oich** can be accessed). Cross over the busy A82 road with care. ▸

After crossing the A82 road, pass the Bridge House Tea Garden and follow a clear track beside the Caledonian Canal. Look across the water to spot a large overspill weir feeding excess water into the River Oich. When **Cullochy Lock** is reached, cross over the lock gates to pick up and follow a track on the other side of the canal, passing several particularly tall and graceful birch trees. The canal broadens considerably where a small loch was incorporated into its course. An overspill weir has to be crossed later; this could mean wet feet if there

A couple of B&Bs can be found by following the main road in either direction, but they lie well off-route and traffic can be very busy.

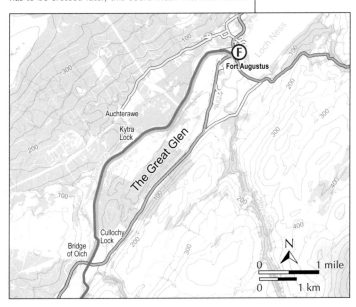

63

The Caledonian Canal is considerably broader after Kytra Lock

A basic 'Trailblazer Rest' campsite is available. A key for the toilet needs to be obtained in advance via the Great Glen Way website or Caledonian Canal office.

is excess water in the canal, though this would be a very rare occurrence.

Pass **Kytra Lock**, where tall pine trees flank the canal on both sides. ◄ The pines soon give way to more mixed woodland cover; there are glimpses of the **River Oich** from time to time as canal and river pursue parallel courses. Hazel trees are abundant beside the track, while later a fine row of pine trees grows along the opposite bank, after the canal bends gradually to the left and passes a power line. Another covered overspill weir is passed, then the canal bends to the right and the buildings of **Fort Augustus** can be seen ahead. The village sits on either side of a fine flight of five locks stepping down towards **Loch Ness**. When the A82 road is reached, turn left in the direction of Inverness. Cross a bridge over the River Oich to reach the tourist information centre.

As walkers descend the flight of five locks through Fort Augustus, metal disks along the way pose all sorts of questions about the Caledonian Canal, its history, construction and use. Visitors who want to find the answers are directed to the **Caledonian Canal Visitor Centre**, just across the road. A small exhibition space can be explored, there are books on sale about the canal, while British Waterways Scotland staff are on hand to deal with any queries. The centre is open 10am–5.30pm, April to October, and entry is free (01320 366493).

FORT AUGUSTUS

The earliest settlement at Fort Augustus (Gaelic – *Cill Chuimein*) was founded in the 6th century by monks from Iona, led by St Cumin. Precious little else is recorded about the place until, in the aftermath of the Jacobite Rising of 1715, a fort was constructed on the site now occupied by the Lovat Hotel. When General Wade built a military road through the area in 1726, the fort was moved to where the Abbey now stands. Fort Augustus was named after William Augustus, Duke of Cumberland, and was destroyed at the beginning of the Jacobite Rising of 1745. 'Butcher' Cumberland had it rebuilt while engaged in a brutal campaign to suppress the Highland clans. In 1876 the site was given to the Benedictines who built the Abbey, vacating it in 1997. The Abbey has since been redeveloped and there is no longer any public access.

The bustling tourist village of Fort Augustus is halfway along the Great Glen Way. It offers plenty of accommodation, from a campsite, hostels and humble B&Bs to fine hotels. There is a bank, and an ATM at the Spar shop. There is a post office and a choice of food and gift shops, several bars, restaurants, cafés and take-aways. Toilets are located beside the tourist information centre (0845 2255121). The Great Glen Way Rangers have an office in the forest at Auchtertawe, not far from Fort Augustus (see Appendix A). There are regular daily bus services to Fort William and Inverness. A variety of cruises on Loch Ness are also available. An interesting rural attraction close to the village is the Highland and Rare Breeds Park, signposted from the bridge, open all year, with an entrance charge, or honesty box when unstaffed (01320 366433).

INVERGARRY LINK

The Invergarry Link allows walkers to vary their journey along the Great Glen Way by passing through the village of Invergarry, instead of walking along the southern shore of Loch Oich. Invergarry offers slightly more in the way of lodgings and facilities than the main route. However, using the link route adds 7.5km (4¾ miles) to the distance covered from Gairlochy on Stage 2, while that to Fort Augustus on Stage 3 becomes 4km (2½ miles) shorter. Overall, using the Invergarry Link means walking 3.5km (2¼ miles) more than the main Great Glen Way route, with 250m (820ft) of extra ascent.

STAGE 2A
Gairlochy to Invergarry

Start	Gairlochy Bottom Lock (NN 176 842)
Finish	Invergarry (NH 307 011)
Distance	26.5km (16½ miles)
Total ascent	480m (1575ft)
Time	6hr 30min
Terrain	Minor roads, forest tracks and paths.
Maps	OS Landranger 34, OS Explorer 400, Harvey Great Glen Way
Refreshments	Shop at the Well of the Seven Heads. Hotel bar/restaurant in Invergarry.
Public Transport	Regular daily Scottish Citylink buses link Invergarry with Fort William, Fort Augustus and Inverness.

After spending a day walking beside Loch Lochy, there are few facilities at Laggan. Some walkers might prefer to switch to the Invergarry Link, which offers a few more facilities. An easy road walk leads towards the Well of the Seven Heads and a handy shop. Forest tracks, including one good view of Loch Oich, are used to continue towards Invergarry. Limited lodgings and bus services are available, while the Glengarry Heritage Centre lies off-route.

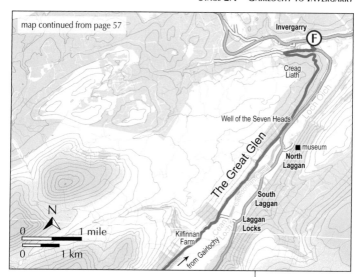

map continued from page 57

Invergarry

Creag
Liath

Well of the Seven Heads

■ museum

North
Laggan

The Great Glen

South
Laggan

Laggan
Locks

Kilfinnan
Farm

from Gairlochy

N

0   1 mile

0   1 km

Follow Stage 2 route description as far as **Kilfinnan Farm**.
After passing the farm, a narrow tarmac road reaches
a junction where the main route heads right for nearby
South Laggan, while the Invergarry Link heads left,
marked for 'Invergarry Services'. The road rises gently,
undulates as it passes a few houses, then descends gently
to the A82 road near **North Laggan**. Turn left and follow
the path parallel to the road, then turn left again onto a
forest track, as marked. ▶

The Well of the Seven Heads marks an historic and
bloody act of retribution. On 25 September 1663,
Alexander MacDonald, Chief of Keppoch, and his
brother Ranald were killed by seven others during
a clan dispute. While most of their kinsfolk seemed
content to let the matter rest, Iain Lom, the Keppoch
Bard, called for revenge, enlisting the support of
MacDonald of Glengarry and Sir James MacDonald
of Sleat. After two years, the seven culprits were
tracked down to Inverlair, where they were slain

For 1:25K route
map see booklet
pages 10–18.

The Well of the Seven
Heads store and Well
of the Seven Heads
monument lie 600
metres further along
the road. Take-away
food is available.

A little house beside the road on the way to Invergarry

and beheaded. The severed heads were washed in a well beside Loch Oich, then displayed at Invergarry Castle before being taken to Gallows Hill in Edinburgh on 7 December 1665. The Well of the Seven Heads is now enclosed in stone and bears a monument crowned with seven unhappy-looking heads, surmounted by a hand holding a dagger. The tale of murder and revenge is carved around all four sides in English, Gaelic, French and Latin.

Walk up the forest track and keep straight ahead at a couple of junctions, gently undulating and gaining a view of **Loch Oich** from a picnic table around 130m (425ft) on the slopes of **Creag Liath**. The track continues through the forest and swings left as it descends, later swinging right to join a narrow tarmac road. Turn right and follow the road past a couple of houses, the Saddle Mountain Hostel and a B&B. When the main A82 road is reached, turn left to follow the pavement, crossing a bridge over the River Garry. Turn left along the A87 into the village of **Invergarry**.

Invergarry (Gaelic – *Inbhir Garadh*) offers a small range of lodgings, including hotels, B&Bs and an independent hostel. Regular daily Scottish Citylink buses link Invergarry with Fort William and Inverness. The Glengarry Heritage Centre is open from Easter to October, on Tuesday, Wednesday and Thursday, 11am–3pm, and can be visited free of charge (01809 501424/511278, www.glengarryheritagecentre.com).

STAGE 3A

Invergarry to Fort Augustus

Start	Invergarry (NH 307 011)
Finish	Tourist Information Centre, Fort Augustus (NH 378 094)
Distance	13.5km (8¼miles)
Total ascent	100m (330ft)
Time	3hr 30min
Terrain	Minor roads, forest tracks and paths.
Maps	OS Landranger 34, OS Explorer 400, Harvey Great Glen Way
Refreshments	Tea garden at Aberchalder Swing Bridge. Plenty of cafés, restaurants, take-aways and bars around Fort Augustus.
Public Transport	Regular daily Scottish Citylink buses link Invergarry with Fort William, Fort Augustus and Inverness

Leaving Invergarry involves a short climb and traverse across a forested slope. Once the main road is reached near the Aberchalder Swing Bridge, it is worth making a short detour to inspect the older, elegant Bridge of Oich. Afterwards, simply re-join the main Great Glen Way, which follows the level track beside the Caledonian Canal. A fine flight of locks finally leads down into Fort Augustus.

To leave **Invergarry**, pass the Invergarry Hotel and a block of houses, then turn right at a telephone kiosk. Follow a winding path uphill, passing tall oaks and rhododendron bushes, which later give way to conifers and rhododendron bushes. Cross a forest track, later joining it again, turning left to follow it gently uphill past **Nursery Wood**. Later, there is a view down to the roof of the Invergarry Power Station. Follow the track downhill and keep straight ahead at a junction, almost reaching a gate and the main A82 road. However, turn left beforehand as marked, along a gravel path following a power line through a broad forest ride. The path rises and falls, crosses a bridge and makes a loop as it crosses a

For 1:25K route map see booklet pages 18–22.

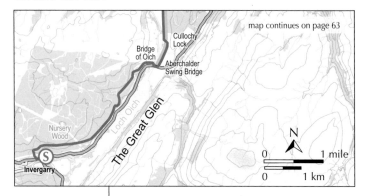

Alternatively, on reaching the swing bridge, turn left to visit the Bridge of Oich, then follow a track beside the Caledonian Canal to re-join the main route of the Great Glen Way at Cullochy Lock.

clear-felled slope. Eventually, drop to the main road, turn left and follow the pavement to the **Aberchalder Swing Bridge**. Cross the road with care to use the safe pedestrian path across the bridge, then cross back over the road to follow a track beside the **Caledonian Canal**. This is the main route of the Great Glen Way. ◄

It is worth leaving the Great Glen Way for a few minutes to reach the **Bridge of Oich**. An older bridge was swept away in devastating floods during 1849, when the embankment of the Caledonian Canal was also breached. Five years elapsed before a new bridge was built, by a brewer-turned-engineer called James Dredge, from Bath. The Bridge of Oich looks like a slender suspension bridge, but was actually patented as a 'double cantilever', built on the 'taper principle'. The supporting chains gradually diminish as they spread outwards from the stout granite pillars that support them, and hold very little weight in the middle of the bridge. Apparently, if the bridge was severed in the middle, it would remain standing. The Bridge of Oich carried traffic up to 1932, but the busy A82 road now crosses a more solid-looking stone bridge nearby.

Follow Stage 3 route description to Fort Augustus.

STAGE 4A

Fort Augustus to Invermoriston (high-level)

Start	Tourist Information Centre, Fort Augustus (NH 378 094)
Finish	Glenmoriston Arms Hotel, Invermoriston (NH 420 168)
Distance	12km (7½ miles)
Total ascent	560m (1840ft)
Time	3hr 15min
Terrain	Forest tracks and upland moorland paths with some short, steep slopes.
Maps	OS Landranger 34, OS Explorer 416S, Harvey Great Glen Way
Refreshments	Invermoriston has a hotel with a bar/restaurant and one other restaurant.
Public Transport	Regular daily Scottish Citylink buses link Fort Augustus and Invermoriston with Inverness and Fort William.

There are two options for linking Fort Augustus with Invermoriston. The high-level route should be open at all times, but in really bad weather it might be wise to take the low-level option (Stage 4B). It isn't particularly difficult, and some walkers might add it to the previous day's walk if they are trying to cover the Great Glen Way in a hurry. Alternatively, the morning could be spent exploring Fort Augustus, or taking a short cruise on Loch Ness in order to gain a greater appreciation of its vastness.

The high-level route of the Great Glen Way climbs above the forested northern slopes of Loch Ness, allowing far more expansive views than are gained from the low-level route. Invermoriston is a tiny village, which can be explored easily in the evening. Alternatively, it is worth looking for fine waterfalls on the lower reaches of the River Moriston. If planning to stay in the village, it is wise to book lodgings in advance, although it is a simple matter to catch a bus elsewhere in search of accommodation.

Leave the tourist information centre in **Fort Augustus** by following the busy **A82** road in the direction of Inverness. Turn left up a minor road called Bunoich Brae (or more

For 1:25K route map see booklet pages 22–26.

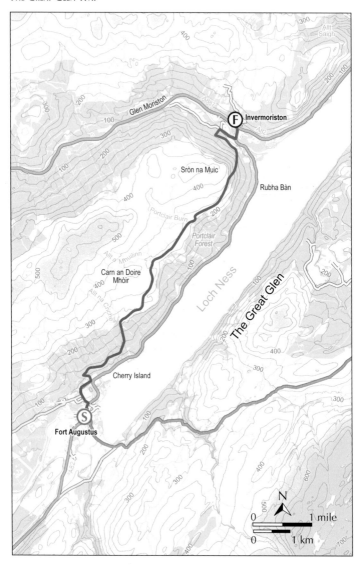

Kytra Lock is on an island between the Caledonian Canal and the River Oich

correctly short-cut up a tarmac path just beforehand). Follow the road uphill, past Morag's Lodge Independent Hostel, keeping straight ahead at a junction. ▶

The narrow road passes a few B&Bs and runs down towards the busy main road. Just before reaching the road, at Three Bridges, turn left along a riverside path. Cross a footbridge in a wood, then climb a steep slope covered in tall, stately pines. Turn right along a forest track and follow it gently downhill, crossing a bridge. There are good views from a noticeboard overlooking the head of **Loch Ness** and **Cherry Island**.

A left turn at the junction, for Jenkins Park and Auchterawe, leads to the Great Glen Way Rangers' base.

LOCH NESS

Walkers see more of Loch Ness from the high-level route; especially when walking above the forest. The deep trough it occupies has been filled with water ever since the end of the Ice Age around 10,000 years ago, and it reflects enough light to brighten even the dullest days in the Great Glen. Six major rivers carry water into Loch Ness, from a part of the Highlands known for high rainfall, explaining why the River Ness flows so powerfully past Inverness. Here are some facts and figures to help appreciate its full extent:

- Catchment area: 1800 sq km (700 square miles)
- Surface area: 56 sq km (21½ square miles)
- Length: 37km (23 miles)
- Width: 3km (2 miles)
- Shoreline length: 86km (53½ miles)
- Volume: 7.5 cu km (1.8 cubic miles)
- Maximum depth: 230m (755ft)
- Surface level: 16m (52ft) above sea level

There is only one island in Loch Ness: the diminutive Cherry Island near Fort Augustus, which is actually an ancient man-made island dwelling, or *crannog*. More astonishing facts include oft-repeated statements that the volume of water in the loch exceeds that of all the lakes and reservoirs in England and Wales, and is sufficient to immerse the entire population of the world!

The high-level route was constructed in 2014, crossing moorland above forested slopes

Follow the track downhill to a junction, where the high-level and low-level routes part, and turn left. The track rises gently and ends at a junction with the way-marked Allt na Criche Trail. Turn left up a gravel path, climbing beside vigorous little waterfalls, later joining

another track. Turn right and cross a bridge over another waterfall on **Allt na Criche**, then turn left up another winding path, glimpsing yet more waterfalls. The path rises from the forest onto a rugged moorland slope of grass, heather and bog myrtle. The path surface is firm, easy and dry, with good drainage.

Reach a viewpoint around 225m (740ft), where there are good views of Loch Ness. The path ahead is very clear, undulating and winding, with a few stone steps leading up and down. Later, pass a stone-built windbreak shelter on a shoulder of **Carn an Doire Mhòir**, around 315m (1035ft), where views of the loch are more extensive. The path winds down into a valley to cross a footbridge over the **Allt a' Mhuilinn**.

The path continues easily across the rugged moorland slopes above the forest, crossing a couple more footbridges. Later, there are two footbridges close together, where there are waterfalls on **Portclair Burn**. Cross yet another footbridge and pass beneath a power line, then briefly touch the edge of the forest. The path traverses the slope and crosses a couple more footbridges, as well as passing a stone bench.

Eventually, the path enters the forest below the rugged face of **Sròn na Muic**, and winds steeply downhill. There are stone steps on some of the bends, then two forest tracks are crossed in quick succession above **Glen Moriston**, as the high-level route re-joins the low-level route, around 90m (295ft).

Turn left and follow an old track running just below the forest track, passing big beech trees, birch and alder, rather than conifers. Either track could be used, but whichever is chosen, it is important to watch for a way-marked path dropping suddenly on the right, winding down a clear-felled slope. Turn right along a road and follow it to a junction with the main A82 road. Turn left, but note the ravaged remains of Telford's Bridge spanning the River Moriston, and the splendid Moriston Falls that spill beneath it. The main road runs into the little village of **Invermoriston**.

The ramshackle remains of **Telford's Bridge**, also known as the Old Bridge, could be crossed in preference to the main road bridge, but take care as the masonry is in a bad state of repair. Despite being nothing more than a standard double-span stone arch, its construction spanned several years from 1805 until 1813, owing to a 'languid and inattentive contractor' and 'idle workers'. The bridge is one of more than a thousand associated with Telford.

THE SEVEN MEN OF GLEN MORISTON

The date was 27 July 1746, when Bonnie Prince Charlie was on the run after the crushing defeat at the Battle of Culloden. Pursued by 'Butcher' Cumberland, and with a bounty of £30,000 on his head, Charles had not eaten for two days and was clad in rags by the time he reached Glen Moriston. Coming upon a crude hut and ravenously hungry, he was warned by his companions not to seek food or shelter in case he was recognised. Charles declared 'I had better be killed like a man than starved like a fool', and made his way to the hut. The seven men inside were mere outlaws, and one of them recognised him, but to their credit, they spurned the chance to claim the bounty and risked their lives to feed and shelter him. Meanwhile, on the road through Glen Moriston, an Edinburgh merchant named Roderick MacKenzie, who bore a passing resemblance to the Bonnie Prince, was shot at by troops. As he died he declared, 'Alas, you have killed your prince', and this ruse was sufficient to buy enough time for Charles to be smuggled out of the country.

Invermoriston (Gaelic – *Inbhir Mor Eason*) has only a few facilities, but at the end of the day these prove most welcome. The Glenmoriston Arms Hotel is very prominent. It was originally a drovers' inn, dating from 1740, and the oldest parts are around the bar and reception area. Johnson and Boswell stayed there while planning a trip to the Hebrides in 1773. There are a few B&Bs in and around the village, as well as the Glenmoriston Stores Post Office, the Clog and Craft Shop, and further along the Skye Road, the Glen Rowan Coffee Shop and Restaurant. Toilets are available inside the Glenmoriston Millennium Hall, when open. Regular daily Scottish Citylink buses link Invermoriston with Inverness and Fort William, as well as the Isle of Skye.

STAGE 4B

Fort Augustus to Invermoriston (low-level)

Start	Tourist Information Centre, Fort Augustus (NH 378 094)
Finish	Glenmoriston Arms Hotel, Invermoriston (NH 420 168)
Distance	12km (7½ miles)
Total ascent	300m (985ft)
Time	3hr
Terrain	Forest tracks and paths with some short, steep slopes.
Maps	OS Landranger 34, OS Explorer 416S, Harvey Great Glen Way
Refreshments	Invermoriston has a hotel with a bar/restaurant and one other restaurant.
Public Transport	Regular daily Scottish Citylink buses link Fort Augustus and Invermoriston with Inverness and Fort William.

Before making firm plans to follow the low-level route from Fort Augustus to Invermoriston please note that it might sometimes be closed for timber harvesting. Check in advance on the Great Glen Way website, and if the route is closed switch to the high-level option (Stage 4A). This is a short day, and some walkers might add it to the previous day's walk if they are trying to cover the Great Glen Way in a hurry. Alternatively, the morning could be spent exploring Fort Augustus, or taking a short cruise on Loch Ness.

The low-level route of the Great Glen Way often runs close to Loch Ness, but the forested slopes usually shield it from view, so walkers see less of it than they might imagine. Invermoriston is a tiny village, which can be explored easily in the evening. Alternatively, it is worth looking for fine waterfalls on the lower reaches of the River Moriston. If planning to stay in the village, it is wise to book lodgings in advance, although it is a simple matter to catch a bus elsewhere in search of accommodation.

Leave the tourist information centre in **Fort Augustus** by following the busy **A82** in the direction of Inverness. Turn left up a minor road called Bunoich Brae (or more

For 1:25K route map see booklet pages 22–26.

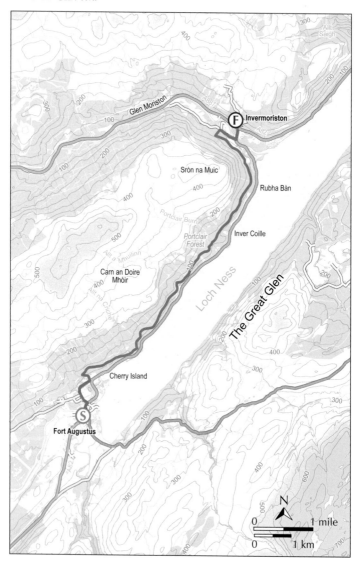

The low-level route generally follows easy forest tracks

correctly short-cut up a tarmac path just beforehand). Follow the road uphill, past Morag's Lodge Independent Hostel, keeping straight ahead at a junction. ▶

The narrow road passes a few B&Bs and runs down towards the busy main road. Just before the road, at Three Bridges, turn left along a riverside path. Cross a footbridge in a wood, then climb a steep slope covered in tall, stately pines. Turn right along a forest track and follow it gently downhill. There are good views from a noticeboard overlooking the head of **Loch Ness** and **Cherry Island**.

Follow the track downhill to junction where the high-level and low-level routes part. Turn right; the track descends gently and leads through a gate, almost back onto the main road. Turn left to follow another track away from the road, quickly swinging right to cross the tumbling stream of **Allt na Criche**.

The woods are mixed, with some fine oaks and birch, but as the broad track bends and climbs, avoiding a left turn, there are more conifers. Pass a gate

A left turn at the junction, for Jenkins Park and Auchterawe, leads to the Great Glen Way Rangers' base.

One of many fine waterfalls passed while following the Allt na Criche.

and climb among tall conifers, with lush margins of heather, bilberry, mosses, ferns and wood sorrel. There is a slight dip in the track, then keep straight ahead at a junction to climb gradually among tall trees on the slopes ofDruim na Garbh Leachtrach. Walk downhill, then uphill, then enjoy good views over a slope of young trees, across **Loch Ness** to the rugged hill of Beinn a' Bhacaidh. Another gentle rise leads to a stone-slab seat, with splendid views both ways along the length of Loch Ness.

Views are lost on a descent into tall forest, where a concrete bridge spans a waterfall on the **Allt a' Mhuilinn**. There is a gentle ascent with a view across a younger part of the forest, again taking in the hill of Beinn a' Bhacaidh across Loch Ness. Walk gently downhill, losing the views. Cross a concrete bridge over **Portclair Burn**, then cross a dip in the track. ◀ Climb gently to cross another concrete bridge over a small waterfall. There is a good view of Loch Ness on the way downhill, overlooking a clear-felled slope, then views

A campsite at Inver Coille is marked off-route, down to the right.

are lost and the gentle descent becomes steeper. The main track suddenly swings sharp right, so keep straight ahead up another track.

The track climbs over a crest and swings left into **Glen Moriston**, and there is another view of Loch Ness after making the turn. Keep right at a junction and almost immediately note the high-level route joining from the left, around 90m (295ft).

Step to the right and follow an old track running just below the forest track, passing big beech trees, birch and alder, rather than conifers. Either track could be used, but whichever is chosen, it is important to watch for a waymarked path dropping suddenly on the right, winding down a clear-felled slope. Turn right along a road and follow it to a junction with the main A82 road. Turn left, but note the ravaged remains of Telford's Bridge spanning the River Moriston, and the splendid Moriston Falls that spill beneath it. The main road runs into the little village of **Invermoriston**. ▶

For information about Invermoriston see Stage 4A.

Telford's Bridge spans the River Moriston and the Falls of Moriston near Invermoriston

STAGE 5A

Invermoriston to Drumnadrochit (high-level)

Start	Glenmoriston Arms Hotel, Invermoriston (NH 420 168)
Finish	Tourist Information Centre, Drumnadrochit (NH 507 299)
Distance	22.5km (14 miles)
Total ascent	710m (2330ft)
Time	5hr 45min
Terrain	Forest tracks and paths with some short, steep slopes. Moorland road.
Maps	OS Landrangers 26 and 34, OS Explorer 416S, Harvey Great Glen Way
Refreshments	Tearoom at a pottery at Grotaig. Plenty of restaurants, cafés and take-aways around Drumnadrochit.
Public Transport	Regular daily Scottish Citylink buses link Invermoriston and Drumnadrochit with Inverness and Fort William. Schooldays-only buses link Grotaig and Drumnadrochit.

There are two options for linking Invermoriston and Drumnadrochit. The high-level route should be open at all times, but in really bad weather it might be wise to take the low-level option (Stage 5B). Despite height being gained, and the route running just outside the forest, there are no views of Loch Ness at first because the hills of Creag nan Eun and Meall na Sròine are in the way. There is an option to switch to the low-level route by walking down a forest track to Alltsigh, otherwise keep climbing to reach the highest point on the Great Glen Way on the slopes of Creag Dhearg. The high-level and low-level routes are reunited shortly afterwards, and both feature good views of Loch Ness.

Bear in mind that a pottery at Grotaig has a tearoom, but otherwise there are no refreshments until Lewiston and Drumnadrochit are reached at the end of the day.

For 1:25K route map see booklet pages 26–32.

Leave **Invermoriston** via the A887, signposted for Kyle of Lochalsh and referred to locally as the Skye Road. Turn right at the Clog and Craft Shop, where a milestone warns

'Last Clog Shop before Skye – 52 miles'. A steep and narrow zigzag road climbs past Craik na Dav B&B, up a well-wooded slope bearing sycamore, beech, oak and birch, with a holly understorey at a higher level. Densely planted conifers flank the road before it crosses a bridge over a stream. Turn right almost immediately to follow a forest track crossing another bridge over the same stream. ▶

A junction is reached, where the high-level and low-level routes part. Turn left along a path which rises to a junction at the corner of a drystone wall. Turn right and keep climbing, with forest to the right and a field to the left. Old birch trees are dotted around on the slopes outside the forest. Walk down a winding path, with stone steps where it gets steeper, and cross a footbridge over a stream.

Before reaching the road/track junction, a steep and winding gravel path offers a short-cut uphill.

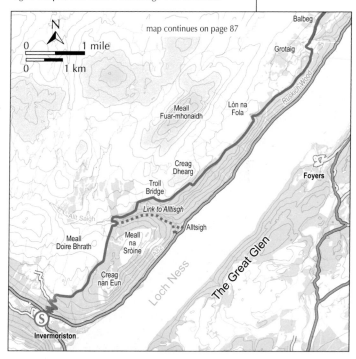

map continues on page 87

83

The high-level route crosses the 'Troll Bridge' above a waterfall

The path climbs and joins a track in a forest that has been partly clear-felled. Turn left to follow the track to a turning space, then continue along a path, noting a curious sculpture on the left, where tree branches have been woven into a circle, mounted on a stone plinth. Follow the path past the little hill of **Meall Doire Bhrath**, around 330m (1080ft), and pass a couple of stone slabs that flank the path like old gateposts. The path descends to a track, and a left turn quickly leads across a concrete bridge spanning **Allt Saigh**. ◀

Turning right down the track leads, in 2km (1¼ miles), to the low-level route at Alltsigh, close to Briarbank B&B, Loch Ness Youth Hostel and bus services.

Follow the track onwards through the forest until it ends, then walk up a winding path that soon runs just outside the forest, beside a tall deer fence. Cross two footbridges; the second one being the rustic **Troll Bridge**, perched above a waterfall. The path climbs and winds further up a steep slope, featuring a few stone steps at one point. Pass a stone-built windbreak shelter, where there is a fine view of Loch Ness. The highest point on the Great Glen Way comes soon afterwards, around 415m (1360ft) on the rugged slopes of **Creag Dhearg**.

The path continues easily, traversing the slopes then drifting into the forest. Follow it downhill, and down a rock step, to reach a junction with a forest track near another stone-built windbreak. Again, there is a fine view of Loch Ness. Turn left along the track, where the slopes have been clear-felled and replanted, leaving occasional sparse Scots pines standing tall, with abundant rosebay willowherb. Looking far across Loch Ness, the remote Monadh Liath range rolls southwards into the distance.

A track junction is reached where the low-level route climbs to re-join the high-level route. Keep left to continue, later crossing a bridge over a waterfall. Follow the track until it ends beyond **Lòn na Fola**, in the forest above **Ruskich Wood**. Continue along a clear path, noting how the forest edges are often softened by birch. Pass a log bench while heading gradually downhill, with only occasional views of Loch Ness.

The path becomes convoluted and passes through gates while running parallel to a track below a fort on the little hill of Dùn Scriben. Emerge from the forest into a field, passing through patchy woodlands before crossing a concrete bridge over Grotaig Burn. Walk up to a road, where the route turns right and passes a small car park. ▶

Turning left leads, in less than 200 metres, to the Loch Ness Clay Works pottery and tearoom at Grotaig.

Follow a path running parallel to the minor road around **Balbeg**. There are occasional glimpses of Loch

Snow on a roadside path above Ancarraig, with a view of Meall Fuar-mhonaidh

Ness while passing isolated houses and farms. Look back to see the humped hills of Meall Fuar-mhonaidh and Creag Dhearg. After the roadside path ends, follow the road past the Ancarraig lodges access, then gorse grows on either side as the road rises up a boggy moorland slope. Later, a swathe of rough grassland lies to the right, while improved pasture lies to the left. The road undulates over 250m (820ft) on a heather moorland, and there is another path running parallel. Follow the road as it runs into a forest and heads gently downhill, then after passing a house at **Woodend**, it falls more steeply.

Turn left as signposted for the Great Glen Way. Go through a gate and walk down a forest track to another gate. Turn right down a broad forest path, which soon turns left. There is a brief glimpse of Drumnadrochit before the path enters a dense part of the forest, later crossing a footbridge to go through a gate. There are further views of the village as the path runs down across a bracken-clad slope dotted with fine oaks. Swing right to reach **Clunebeg Lodge**, restaurant and B&B. Follow the access track downhill from Clunebeg House, admiring tall beech and oaks alongside.

Walkers who wish to reach the campsite at Borlum, or the celebrated ruins of Urquhart Castle, should turn right and follow the path running parallel to the main road.

The track levels out beside the bouldery River Coiltie. Houses seen on the far side are part of the village of Lewiston. A variety of densely packed trees usually screen the river from view as the track runs to join a minor road at a sign for the Clunebeg Estate. Follow the road straight ahead to reach a picnic area at a junction with the busy A82 road. ◄

Urquhart Castle is 2km (1¼ miles) off-route, or 3.25km (2 miles) from Drumnadrochit, perched on Strone Point overlooking Loch Ness. It can be reached safely on foot as there is a path beside the busy A82 road, and Scottish Citylink buses serve both Drumnadrochit and the castle. The situation is splendid and it is a renowned place for those keeping a lookout for the Loch Ness 'monster'! Once one of the largest castles in Scotland, Urquhart Castle's sprawling ruins take time to explore. A visitor centre offers a thorough grounding in its construction and history, plus a café. Urquhart Castle is open all year and is an entrance charge (01456 450551). For more information, see Stage 5B.

Turn left to follow the A82 road across the River Coiltie to pass though **Lewiston**. Signs alert walkers to offers of food, drink and accommodation, then the road bends gradually right, passing a take-away and supermarket, where there is an ATM, to reach the nearby village of **Drumnadrochit**, which has a greater range of services.

Drumnadrochit (Gaelic – *Druim na Drochaid*) is a busy little village with plenty to catch the attention of passing tourists. Two attractions vying for attention are Nessieland, beside the Loch Ness Hotel, open all year (01456 450342, **www.nessieland.co.uk**), and the Loch Ness Centre & Exhibition at the Drumnadrochit Hotel,

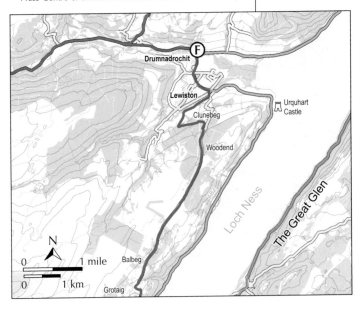

Drumnadrochit appears surrounded by woodland in this distant view

open all year (01456 450573, **www.lochness.com**). There are entrance charges to both places. Whatever you want to know about Loch Ness and its 'monster', this is the place to take on board all the opinions, then you can make up your own mind. If nothing more than a 'Nessie' souvenir is required, a handful of gift shops around the village deal in the widest selection of products.

There is accommodation to suit every pocket, from hotels to guest houses and B&Bs, with an independent hostel in Lewiston and a campsite further along the road at Borlum. Most facilities are clustered round the village green at Drumnadrochit. There is a bank with an ATM, a post office store, toilets, bars, restaurants, cafés and take-aways. There are souvenir and gift shops, as well as a tourist information centre (01456 459086). Regular daily Scottish Citylink buses link Drumnadrochit with Inverness and Fort William. Cruises on Loch Ness are also available (www.lochness-cruises.com).

STAGE 5B

Invermoriston to Drumnadrochit (low-level)

Start	Glenmoriston Arms Hotel, Invermoriston (NH 420 168)
Finish	Tourist Information Centre, Drumnadrochit (NH 507 299)
Distance	23.5km (14½ miles)
Total ascent	600m (1970ft)
Time	5hr 30min
Terrain	Forest tracks and paths, only occasionally steep. Moorland road.
Maps	OS Landrangers 26 and 34, OS Explorer 416S, Harvey Great Glen Way
Refreshments	Snacks at Briarbank B&B at Alltsigh. Tearoom at a pottery at Grotaig. Plenty of restaurants, cafés and take-aways around Drumnadrochit.
Public Transport	Regular daily Scottish Citylink buses link Invermoriston and Drumnadrochit with Inverness and Fort William, and these services can also be accessed at Loch Ness Youth Hostel at Alltsaigh. Schooldays-only buses link Grotaig and Drumnadrochit.

Before making firm plans to follow the low-level route from Invermoriston to Drumnadrochit please note that it might sometimes be closed for timber harvesting. Check in advance on the Great Glen Way website, and if the route is closed switch to the high-level option (Stage 4A). This low-level route is easier, but it is also slightly longer. Most of the day's walk is spent close to Loch Ness, but the slopes are densely forested and there are only occasional views. This will change as more and more areas are clear-felled. As the route climbs higher, it re-joins the high-level route and continues to Grotaig, where Loch Ness passes from view. Walkers continue beside or along a road most of the way to Lewiston and Drumnadrochit.

Two attractions feature at the end of the day, where rival exhibitions are devoted to Loch Ness and its 'monster'. Be sure to arrive in good time if intending to visit either or both of these places, as they are packed with plenty of interest.

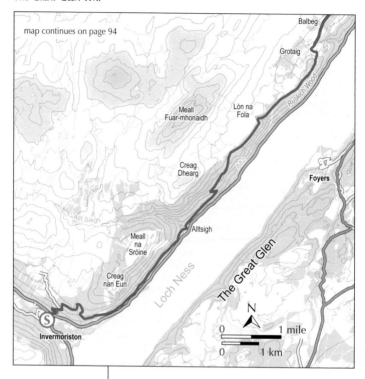

map continues on page 94

Balbeg

Grotaig

Rubha Wood

Meall
Fuar-mhonaidh

Lòn na
Fola

Creag
Dhearg

Foyers

Allt Saigh

Alltsigh

Meall
na
Sròine

Loch Ness

The Great Glen

Creag
nan Eun

N

0 _____ 1 mile

0 _____ 1 km

S
Invermoriston

For 1:25K route
map see booklet
pages 26–32.

Before reaching the
road/track junction,
a steep and winding
gravel path offers a
short-cut uphill.

Leave **Invermoriston** via the A887, signposted for Kyle
of Lochalsh, referred to locally as the Skye Road. Turn
right at the Clog and Craft Shop, where a milestone
warns 'Last Clog Shop before Skye – 52 miles'. A steep
and narrow zigzag road climbs past Craik na Dav B&B,
up a well-wooded slope bearing sycamore, beech, oak
and birch, with a holly understorey at a higher level.
Densely planted conifers flank the road before it crosses
a bridge over a stream. Turn right almost immediately
to follow a forest track crossing another bridge over the
same stream. ◀

A junction is reached, where the low-level and high-
level routes part. Keep straight ahead along the track

to cross a crest, where a thinner part of the plantation reveals some of the former heather cover and low rocky outcrops.

The track swings left, then right, to cross a concrete bridge over a stream. Follow the track through a tall gateway, then turn right downhill from a junction. Turn right at another junction as marked, but also consider turning left as signposted for a nearby viewpoint. This short detour reveals a narrow path winding up a slope covered in ling and bell heather to reach the crude 'Stone Seat', where there is a fine view over **Loch Ness**. The village of Invermoriston, despite being close at hand, is completely hidden from view. Retrace your steps to the junction.

Walk down a narrow and bendy forest path as marked, landing on a forest track below. Turn left and follow the track gently downhill, with only occasional glimpses of Loch Ness. A post draws attention to the 'Stone Cave', said to have been built to offer shelter to a washerwoman on her frequent journeys between Alltsigh and Invermoriston. It still offers splendid shelter. Later,

The 'Stone Cave' was built to offer shelter to a washerwoman

there is a slight climb to a bend where there is a good viewpoint revealing the length of Loch Ness, but also turn around and admire the fine variety of trees stacked against the cliffs of **Creag nan Eun**.

It is possible to turn left at the junction, walk up the track, and link with the high-level route.

Continue down the track, passing a rugged slope of gorse bushes where no forest trees were ever planted, losing views of the loch. Keep straight ahead at a track junction beside a rock cutting, climbing gently for a while. ◄ Walk gently downhill, uphill, then downhill along a track fringed with broom. Drop more steeply from a junction of tracks and cross a concrete bridge over a rocky gorge at **Alltsigh**. There is a waterfall in the gorge, as well as a variety of trees, while a diligent search reveals an old packhorse bridge.

A view of Loch Ness and Beinn a' Bhacaidh from a point near Alltsaigh and the Loch Ness Youth Hostel

For Alltsigh a sign simply states SYHA and points down a track and through a gate. The track passes a white house and quickly reaches the busy A82 road beside Loch Ness. Immediately to the left is Briarbank B&B, which also offers snacks and drinks, while further away to the right is Loch Ness Youth Hostel and a bus stop. The hostel occupies a site offering splendid views across the loch.

Those who don't need to detour to Alltsigh can simply walk straight up a forest track as marked, climbing among tall conifers with no views. Later, there are good views back through the Great Glen. The track bends sharp left and sharp right as it climbs, with views through the glen becoming even more extensive, as well as taking in the village of Foyers across the loch.

The track bends quickly left and right to climb further, then there is another sharp left and sharp right turn, where views through the Great Glen stretch far beyond Fort Augustus to reveal a glimpse of distant Loch Oich. Looking far across Loch Ness, the remote Monadh Liath range rolls southwards into the distance. Clear-felled slopes are profusely covered in rosebay willowherb, with a few Scots pines standing tall.

The high-level route joins from the left, but continue walking straight ahead, later crossing a bridge over a waterfall. Follow the track until it ends beyond **Lòn na Fola**, in the forest above **Ruskich Wood**. Continue along a clear path, noting how the forest edges are often softened by birch. Pass a log bench while heading gradually downhill, with only occasional views of Loch Ness.

The path becomes convoluted and passes through gates while running parallel to a track below a fort on the little hill of Dùn Scriben. Emerge from the forest into a field, passing through patchy woodlands before crossing a concrete bridge over Grotaig Burn. Walk up to a road, where the route turns right and passes a small car park. ▶

Turning left leads, in less than 200 metres, to the Loch Ness Clay Works pottery and tearoom at Grotaig.

Follow a path running parallel to the minor road around **Balbeg**. There are occasional glimpses of Loch Ness while passing isolated houses and farms. Look back to see the humped hills of Meall Fuar-mhonaidh and Creag Dhearg. After the roadside path ends, follow the road past the Ancarraig lodges access, then gorse grows on either side as the road rises up a boggy moorland slope. Later, a swathe of rough grassland lies to the right, while improved pasture lies to the left. The road undulates over 250m (820ft) on a heather moorland, and there is another path running parallel. Follow the road as it runs into a forest and heads gently

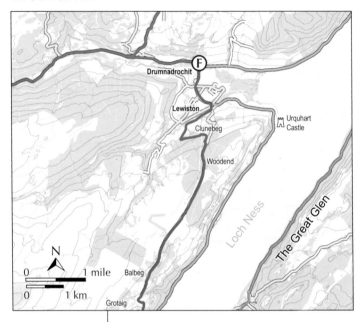

Drumnadrochit

Lewiston

Clunebeg

Urquhart
Castle

Woodend

Loch Ness

The Great Glen

N

0   1 mile

0   1 km

Balbeg

Grotaig

downhill, then after passing a house at **Woodend**, it falls more steeply.

Turn left as signposted for the Great Glen Way. Go through a gate and walk down a forest track to another gate. Turn right down a broad forest path, which soon turns left. There is a brief glimpse of Drumnadrochit before the path enters a dense part of the forest, later crossing a footbridge to go through a gate. There are further views of the village as the path runs down across a bracken-clad slope dotted with fine oaks. Swing right to reach **Clunebeg Lodge**, restaurant and B&B. Follow the access track downhill from Clunebeg House, admiring tall beech and oaks alongside.

The track levels out beside the bouldery River Coiltie. Houses seen on the far side are part of the village of Lewiston. A variety of densely packed trees usually screen the river from view as the track runs to join a minor road at a big sign for the Clunebeg Estate. Follow the road straight ahead to reach a picnic area at a junction with the busy A82 road. ▶

Turn left to follow the A82 road across the River Coiltie to reach **Lewiston**. Signs alert walkers to offers of food, drink and accommodation, then the road bends gradually right, passing a take-away and supermarket, where there is an ATM, to reach the nearby village of **Drumnadrochit**, which has a greater range of services. For information about Drumnadrochit see Stage 5A.

Walkers who wish to reach the campsite at Borlum, or the celebrated ruins of Urquhart Castle, should turn right and follow the path running parallel to the main road.

URQUHART CASTLE

Urquhart Castle is 2km (1¼ miles) off-route, or 3.25km (2 miles) from Drumnadrochit, perched on Strone Point overlooking Loch Ness. It can be reached safely on foot as there is a path beside the busy A82 road, and Scottish Citylink buses serve both Drumnadrochit and the castle. Once one of the largest castles in Scotland, Urquhart Castle's sprawling ruins take time to explore. A visitor centre offers a thorough grounding in its construction and history, plus a café. Urquhart Castle is open all year and there is an entrance charge (01456 450551).

The tower house at Urquhart Castle is a popular place for visitors to keep a lookout for the Loch Ness 'monster'

A Bronze Age promontory fort once stood on Strone Point, and there were other defensive structures on the site before Urquhart Castle was built in the 13th century. Its history is one of intense conflict, in which English and Scots alternately occupied it, with William Wallace and Robert the Bruce each holding the property for a time. Buchan, son of Robert II, held the castle from 1390, ruling with brutal force, and frequently robbing churches. In the 15th and 16th centuries the MacDonalds launched raids on the castle, which was later held by the Grants. The bulk of the damage to the castle was done with explosives in 1692, which prevented it becoming a Jacobite stronghold in subsequent years. Visitors cross a wooden gangway across a defensive ditch, and pass through a gatehouse. However, in the past, most people approaching the castle would have done so through a watergate from Loch Ness. The centrepiece of Urquhart Castle is a stout and impressive tower house, but be sure to take note of the complex arrangement of the ruined defensive walls that surround the site. The best vantage point is of course from the top of the tower house.

A floral model of Urquhart Castle in the middle of Drumnadrochit

Walkers who can't spare the time to detour to the castle can console themselves by studying an interesting floral model of the castle in the middle of the village green in Drumnadrochit.

STAGE 6
Drumnadrochit to Inverness

Start	Tourist Information Centre, Drumnadrochit (NH 507 299)
Finish	Inverness Castle (NH 666 451)
Distance	30.5km (19 miles)
Total ascent	500m (1640ft)
Time	8hr
Terrain	Road, forest and moorland tracks, then urban pathways through green spaces to the finish.
Maps	OS Landranger 26, OS Explorer 416N, Harvey Great Glen Way
Refreshments	Basic campsite café near Abriachan. Plenty of choice in Inverness.
Public Transport	Regular daily Scottish Citylink buses link Drumnadrochit with Inverness and Fort William. Approaching Inverness, there are several points where local city bus services can be accessed. Long-distance bus and rail services are available, and there is an airport nearby.

This is the longest day's walk on the Great Glen Way, and a high point is crossed around 380m (1245ft) in the Abriachan Forest. The forest is managed by the local community, who have cleared, marked and signposted a network of trails. The area is proving popular with visitors and school parties. This is a long stage and the only place it can be broken easily is at an eco-campsite near Abriachan. The route is rather distant from the Great Glen and follows the course of an old drove road, which passes through an interesting remnant Scots pine forest. By the time the route descends back into the glen, it is on the outskirts of Inverness. Take care over route-finding through the suburbs, where one green space after another is linked to provide a route into the very heart of the city.

Once the finish is reached at Inverness Castle, there is a chance to look back along the route through the Great Glen and reflect on your journey across Scotland.

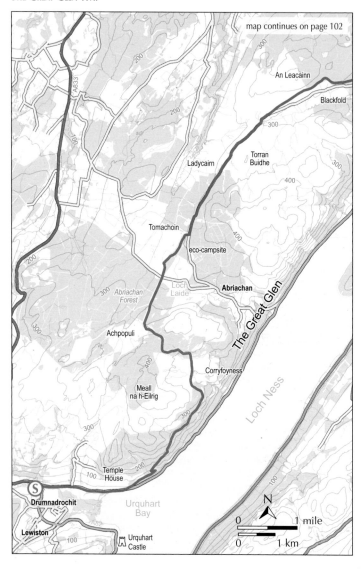

map continues on page 102

An Leacainn

Blackfold

Torran
Buidhe

Ladycairn

Tomachoin

eco-campsite

Loch
Laide

Abriachan

The Great Glen

Abriachan
Forest

Achpopuli

Corryfoyness

Loch Ness

Meall
na h-Eilrig

Temple
House

Ⓢ
Drumnadrochit

Lewiston

Urquhart
Bay

Urquhart
Castle

N

0 — 1 mile
0 — 1 km

Leave **Drumnadrochit** by following the main A82 in the direction of Inverness. Stay on the pavement on the left-hand side throughout, passing a handful of B&B places. There is access on the other side of the road for **Urquhart Bay** Harbour, for cruises on Loch Ness.

For 1:25K route map see booklet pages 32–41.

> **John Cobb** broke land and water speed records. In 1947 his land speed record stood a little short of 400mph (645kph). On 29 September 1952 he achieved a speed of 206mph (331kph) on Loch Ness, from Urquhart Bay. Unfortunately, his craft *Crusader* disintegrated and sank, taking Cobb's life, and the engine wasn't recovered for 50 years.

Turn left up the access road for **Temple House**, then quickly turn left again, up through a gate, to follow a path beside a tall fence to pass the house. There is a brief glimpse of Urquhart Castle across Urquhart Bay on Loch Ness. The path runs parallel to the road, then climbs through small gates and crosses a narrow access road that leads up to Tychat. Continue through woods, climbing through more small gates, then follow a path across a grassy slope overlooking a stretch of Loch Ness, again with a view of **Urquhart Castle**.

A gate leads into dense forest, but the path is clear and obvious. There is a brief glimpse of **Loch Ness** just before a footbridge, then the path climbs gradually. Little light reaches the forest floor, so only moss and wood sorrel grow alongside the path. When the path turns sharply left and right, it climbs through a more open area of grass and bracken, with several birch trees. The path runs more or less level for a while, then climbs, before descending to cross stepping stones over a small burn. A short ascent leads onto a forest track.

Follow the track onwards, undulating at first, then climbing gradually up a clear-felled slope. There are views over Loch Ness, but they aren't particularly good, and at a higher level the track drifts well away from the loch. Go through a tall gate, out of the forest, onto hummocky moorland with a view of isolated buildings at

Corryfoyness, which was once a farm. There are boggy hollows spiked with rushes, as well as heathery humps, and scattered birch trees. The track meanders and climbs gradually to a gateway into another forest.

Signs inform visitors that this is managed by the Abriachan Forest Trust, and there are leaflets available detailing the Abriachan Forest Walks. The Great Glen Way is waymarked as usual, but signposts also point back to Drumnadrochit and ahead to Inverness. The track meanders and reaches a high point around 380m (1245ft). ◄ There is a fairly steep descent to a building near **Achpopuli**, then the track swings right and leads straight down along a broad forest ride. The is part of an old drove road, and towards the end there is access on the right to a car park and a grass-roofed toilet block, along with plenty of information about the Abriachan Forest Walks.

This was the highest point on the Great Glen Way until new high-level options were opened in 2014.

Abriachan is only a small community of around 120 people, yet in the mid-1990s they managed to raise over £150,000 to buy a substantial part of the **Abriachan Forest**. At the time, it was the largest community forest in Scotland, and it has been developed with public access and conservation foremost. A network of walking and cycling trails has been established, as well as a car park

Light snowfall on a forest track high above Abriachan

complete with a picnic site, an eco-toilet and plenty of information. Interesting features just off the course of the Great Glen Way include Loch Laide and the Caiplich Prehistoric Settlement. Visitors can become Friends of the Abriachan Forest Trust, and receive a newsletter keeping them in touch with developments. Pick up a leaflet in the forest or check the website **www.abriachan.org.uk** for full contact details.

Keep straight ahead and the track leaves the forest, with a view of little **Loch Laide** to the right. Cross a minor road and go through a kissing gate to follow a narrow, but clear and obvious gravel path. This path rises gently up a moorland slope dotted with trees, meandering and clipping the corner of a forest. Numerous signs point to the right, where an **eco-campsite** also offers a café and a basic trail cabin for hire, just off-route. As the path approaches the whitewashed house of Woodend, it turns right and runs up to a kissing gate and a minor road, next to a sign for Caiplich Farm.

Turn left and follow the road through a forest, where there are a couple of houses tucked away at **Tomachoin** and Rinuden. The roadside margins often feature birch, willow and rowan. The road runs out of the forest and passes a huddle of houses at **Ladycairn**, then crosses a heathery slope where a number of Scots pines grow. Although the road is fenced, it crosses broad and open moorland covered with ling and bell heather. There are views northwards towards the sprawling slopes of Ben Wyvis, but these are lost once the road crosses a crest over 300m (985ft). The road crosses a stream, then a clear and obvious gritty path heads left, across open moorland on the slopes of **An Leacainn**. The path passes a number of stones carved with 'Dochgarroch' and later links with forest tracks just above **Blackfold**.

Continue as signposted along a track, then quickly turn right as marked through a kissing gate, into tall forest with no views. A sign reminds walkers that they are still following an old drove road, where cattle were driven

A lek is a site where rare black grouse traditionally gather at dawn during spring and autumn to perform noisy courtship displays. As a consequence, dogs should be kept under control.

from west to east, from the Highlands to Inverness. The route passes through ancient pinewoods that are being regenerated, and the sign also draws the attention of walkers to a nearby 'lek'. ◄

Follow the track into the forest and turn left at a junction to stay on the main track. The forest floor is grassy, heathery and mossy, with areas of bilberry. The track meanders and undulates slightly near **Craig Leach**, passing a kissing gate before heading more noticeably downhill. Old drystone walls flank the drove road and the ruin of an old 'lairage', once used as a lodging by drovers, is passed just before a couple of prominent horse chestnut trees.

Moss, heather and bilberry grow thick on top of the flanking walls, and plenty of slender birch and rowan trees grow alongside, often obscuring the ranks of conifers

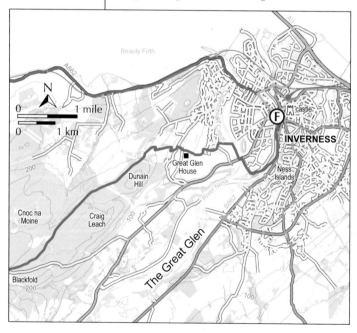

beyond. After passing beneath power lines, look out to the right to spot some fine examples of Scots pines on **Dunain Hill**, and also look to the left, between the birch trees, to glimpse the waters of the **Beauly Firth**; a sure sign that this walk across Scotland is drawing to a conclusion.

Go through a kissing gate and follow a broader track downhill, but turn right at a track junction to pass a pylon and go through an old gateway. Walk out of the woods, through a kissing gate on the left, and cross a dam holding a pond in place. There is a view of Inverness in the distance, then as the path climbs up a grassy slope, there are fine views of the stone-built Creag Dunain Hospital closer to hand. The path runs down a grassy slope and bends to the right to reach a kissing gate. Turn left down a track, passing a variety of trees, including stout beech and towering Scots pines. The track is grassy as it bends right to a kissing gate to reach a road and a Great Glen Way signpost in the grounds of Creag Dunain.

Built in 1864, **Creag Dunain** was originally a huge Victorian mental hospital. By all accounts, its management was progressive and doctors were willing to practise the latest forms of treatment on their patients. The building was later used as a general hospital. In recent years it has been closed and the site is awaiting redevelopment. The Great Glen Way weaves its way between the buildings on its way into the city.

Turn left down the road as marked, then left, right and left again to pass a small gate-lodge building. Turn right as signposted for the Great Glen Way, and note the **Great Glen House** to the right. ▶ Continue as marked and pick up a clear gravel path winding downhill between fields, with rampant hedgerows alongside. The path swings left beside some houses, then there is a right turn down through a broad and grassy space between houses. Cross a road to go through another grassy space, and drift left as marked to cross a road-end and go through an underpass beneath a busy road with bus stops.

This is essentially an office block, but there are 'Paths for All' and other interesting publications available at reception. Energy-efficient and eco-friendly, it won an award for 'Sustainable Building of the Year' in 2006.

Great Glen House is an award-winning eco-building

Follow a paved path, then turn right alongside a golf course and follow a path along an embankment between the golf course and sports pitches. Steps lead up to the **Caledonian Canal**. Turn right to follow a tarmac track parallel, bearing in mind that this is actually running roughly in the direction of Fort William! Turn left across a swing bridge on the busy A82 road, then cross with care. There are buses along this road, as well as the Hebrides B&B.

Do not follow the canal path, or the road running alongside, but follow the path marked as the Great Glen Way, running parallel to the road. Head diagonally left through the car park of the Inverness Sports Centre, then turn right at the Floral Hall and coffee shop. Turn left to walk alongside another road, crossing over it to keep left of a toilet block near Whin Park.

Turn left as marked along a tarmac path, then when the path runs alongside the **River Ness** turn right to cross a white suspension footbridge onto the **Ness Islands**. Turn left alongside the river again, then right across a curved footbridge, which has a small island in its middle. Keep right along another path, then when the island tapers out, turn right across another suspension footbridge. Turn left to walk alongside the **River Ness**, but turn right later to cross a short footbridge over a narrow water channel running parallel.

Turn left alongside the river and follow it into **Inverness**. The popular path is known as Ladies' Walk as far as a suspension footbridge, then it becomes Ness Bank. Watch out for a right turn away from the river, along an alley beside Ness Bank House. Climb up a few steps and turn left up the road called View Place to reach **Inverness Castle**.

Castle Hill rises proudly above the River Ness and is obviously a strategic location. It may have been settled and fortified throughout history, but there was certainly a timber fort there in the 11th century. A stone fort was built in the 12th century, which was rebuilt in the 15th century. **Inverness Castle** was extensively damaged at the end of the Jacobite Rebellion in 1746. The neo-Norman castle, of well-dressed red sandstone, was built in 1834 as

Looking along the River Ness from Ness Islands towards the Cathedral in Inverness

the Sheriff Court and still functions as such today. Outside the castle a statue of Flora MacDonald gazes towards the Great Glen. She was imprisoned in London for helping Bonnie Prince Charlie. Part of the building is equipped as the Castle Garrison Encounter and can be visited (01463 243363).

The Great Glen Way finishes at a stone monument overlooking the River Ness and the later stages of the route. Spend a while looking back towards the Great Glen, then give some thought to how you will spend your remaining time in Inverness.

Behind Inverness Castle is the Castle Wynd, which leads down past toilets to the tourist information centre and the High Street. Walkers will naturally find themselves exploring at least a small part of the city centre, even if they only want to head for the train or bus station. Those who stay overnight will have more time at their disposal and can enjoy further explorations of the city (see 'Last/First night: Inverness' in the Introduction).

THE GREAT GLEN WAY
NORTH TO SOUTH

*Inverness Castle, built of striking red sandstone,
crowns a grassy hill in the very heart of Inverness*

STAGE 1
Inverness to Drumnadrochit

Start	Inverness Castle (NH 666 451)
Finish	Tourist Information Centre, Drumnadrochit (NH 507 299)
Distance	30.5km (19 miles)
Total ascent	540m (1770ft)
Time	8hr
Terrain	Urban pathways through green spaces, followed by forest and moorland tracks and roads.
Maps	OS Landranger 26, OS Explorer 416N, Harvey Great Glen Way
Refreshments	Plenty of choice in Inverness. Basic campsite café at Abriachan. Plenty of restaurants, cafés and take-aways in Drumnadrochit.
Public Transport	Local city bus services around Inverness. Regular daily Scottish Citylink buses link Inverness with Drumnadrochit and Fort William.

This is the longest stage on the Great Glen Way, and there is a fine view from Inverness Castle towards the Great Glen. Take care over route-finding through the city suburbs, where one green space after another leads the walker towards the countryside. The route actually drifts away from the Great Glen, following the course of an old drove road through an interesting remnant Scots pine forest. A road walk leads towards an eco-campsite near Abriachan, the only place this long day's walk could be broken. Abriachan Forest is managed by the local community, who have cleared, marked and signposted a network of trails. The area is proving popular with visitors and school parties, and a high point on the Great Glen Way is crossed around 380m (1245ft).

Drumnadrochit is reached at the end of the day, where the principal attractions are two rival exhibitions devoted to Loch Ness and its 'monster'.

For 1:25K route map see booklet pages 32–41.

Walkers starting at either the railway station or bus station in **Inverness** will have to negotiate the busy city streets for a few minutes to find **Inverness Castle**. This is prominently located on a green hill just behind the Town House

and tourist information centre, overlooking the powerful flow of the River Ness. A stone monument marks the start of the Great Glen Way, and the route is marked throughout with signs bearing a 'thistle' logo.

Inverness Castle was built as the Sheriff Court and still functions as such today

Castle Hill rises proudly above the River Ness and is obviously a strategic location. It may have been settled and fortified throughout history, but there was certainly a timber fort there in the 11th century. A stone fort was built in the 12th century, which was rebuilt in the 15th century. **Inverness Castle** was extensively damaged at the end of the Jacobite Rebellion in 1746. The neo-Norman castle seen today, of well-dressed red sandstone, was built in 1834. Outside the castle a statue of Flora MacDonald gazes towards the Great Glen. She was imprisoned in London for helping Bonnie Prince Charlie. Part of the building is equipped as the Castle Garrison Encounter and can be visited (01463 243363).

Walk down the road called View Place, and cross a busy road. Almost immediately, turn right down some

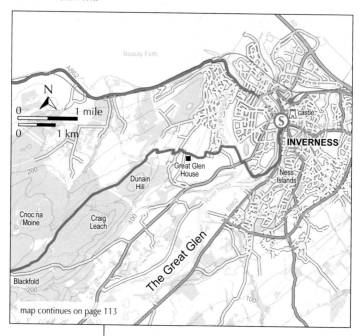

Great Glen House

Dunain Hill

Cnoc na Moine

Craig Leach

Blackfold

The Great Glen

Beauly Firth

INVERNESS

Castle

Ness Islands

River Ness

map continues on page 113

stone steps and walk through an alley beside Ness Bank House, to reach the **River Ness**. Turn left along a popular riverside path, known as Ness Bank until it reaches a white suspension footbridge, where it becomes Ladies' Walk. Continue beside the river, then cross a short footbridge on the right, which spans a narrow water channel, then turn left to walk between the channel and the river. Turn right to cross a suspension footbridge onto the **Ness Islands**, then turn left and keep left. Later, cross a curved footbridge, which has a small island in its middle, and turn left to walk alongside the river again. Turn right over another suspension footbridge, then turn left to follow the river, and a narrow channel, to a toilet block near Whin Park.

Cross over a road and look for a path running parallel to it, to reach a nearby road junction. Turn right to reach the Floral Hall and coffee shop, then turn left and walk diagonally left through the car park of the Inverness Sports Centre. Look for markers to find another path running parallel to a road, then turn left at the Hebrides B&B to follow the busy A82 road across a swing bridge on the **Caledonian Canal**. ▶

The A82 road has bus services.

Turn right to follow a clear tarmac track beside the canal, which actually leads back towards Inverness! However, there are steps down to the left, leading onto a path following an embankment between a golf course and sports pitches. Keep straight ahead and later turn left along a paved path, which goes through an underpass beneath a busy road with bus stops.

Walk past a road-end, then drift right across a grassy area as marked, looking for a grassy space between houses. Cross a road and walk gently up through another broader grassy space between houses. Turn left along a path behind some houses, then drift right as marked to follow a clear gravel path winding uphill between fields, with rampant hedgerows alongside. Follow the markers along a road, with the **Great Glen House** to the left, to reach a road junction. ▶ Turn left past the former Creag Dunain Hospital to reach a small gate-lodge building. Turn right, left, and right again as marked, to find the Great Glen Way signposted on the right at the edge of the hospital grounds. The fiddly route-finding through the suburbs of Inverness is over, and ahead lies more open countryside.

Great Glen House is essentially an office block, but there are 'Paths for All' and other interesting publications available at reception. Energy-efficient and eco-friendly, it won an award for 'Sustainable Building of the Year' in 2006.

Built in 1864, **Creag Dunain** was originally a huge Victorian mental hospital. By all accounts, its management was progressive and doctors were willing to practise the latest forms of treatment on their patients. The building was later used as a general hospital. In recent years it has been closed and the site is awaiting redevelopment. The Great Glen Way weaves its way between the buildings on its way out of the city.

Go through a kissing gate and follow a clear, grassy track as it bends left uphill past towering Scots pines and stout beech. Turn right through another kissing gate and follow a clear path uphill. It bends to the left and runs up across a grassy slope, enjoying fine views of the stone-built hospital below. Follow the path down another grassy slope and look back towards Inverness, which will soon be lost to view. Cross a dam holding a pond in place, go through a kissing gate and turn right along a woodland track across the slopes of **Dunain Hill**. Go through an old gateway and past a pylon, then turn left up a broader track. Go through a kissing gate onto yet another track.

A sign reminds walkers that they are following an old drove road, where cattle were driven from west to east, from the Highlands to Inverness. The route passes through ancient pinewoods that are being regenerated on **Craig Leach**, and the sign also draws the attention of walkers to a nearby 'lek'. ◄ Look out to the left to spot Scots pines, and to the right, between birch trees, to glimpse the waters of the **Beauly Firth**.

A lek is a site where rare black grouse traditionally gather at dawn during spring and autumn to perform noisy courtship displays. As a consequence, dogs should be kept under control.

Pass under power lines and note slender birch and rowan trees growing alongside, often obscuring the ranks of conifers beyond. Moss, heather and bilberry grow thick on top of the old drystone walls that flank the track. Just after passing a couple of prominent chestnut trees, the ruin of an old 'lairage' is passed, once used by drovers. The track rises to a kissing gate, then meanders and undulates slightly without its flanking drystone walls. The forest floor is grassy, heathery and mossy, with areas of bilberry. Turn right at a junction to stay on the main track, and eventually go through a final kissing gate where views begin to open up.

Cross a forest track just above **Blackfold** and pick up a gritty path that crosses open moorland on the slopes of **An Leacainn**, where there is ling and bell heather. The path passes a number of stones carved with 'Dochgarroch' and later descends gently to a minor road. Turn right to cross a stream; the road crosses a crest over 300m (985ft), with views northwards towards the sprawling slopes of Ben Wyvis. After crossing a heathery slope where a number of Scots pines grow, the road passes

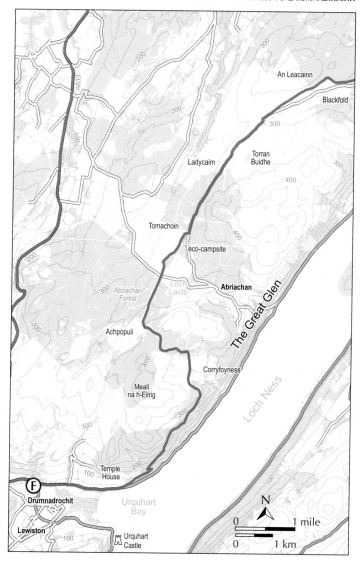

a huddle of houses at **Ladycairn**. The roadside margins often feature birch, willow and rowan on the way through a forest, and there are a couple of houses tucked away at **Tomachoin** and Rinuden. Watch out for a sign for Caiplich Farm, and go through a kissing gate on the right to leave the road.

A clear and obvious gravel path runs downhill and swings left in view of a white house called Woodend. Numerous signs point left, where an **eco-campsite** also offers a café and a basic trail cabin for hire, just off-route. The path clips the corner of a forest and descends gently down a moorland slope dotted with trees, meandering before running straight to a kissing gate onto a minor road. Walk straight ahead along a forest track, with a view of little **Loch Laide** to the left. Also to the left, a little later, is access to a car park and a grass-roofed toilet block, along with plenty of information about the Abriachan Forest Walks.

One of many signs directing walkers off-route to an eco-campsite and café

Abriachan is only a small community of around 120 people, yet in the mid-1990s they managed to raise over £150,000 to buy a substantial part of the **Abriachan Forest**. At the time, it was the largest community forest in Scotland, and it has been developed with public access and conservation foremost. A network of walking and cycling trails has been established, as well as a car park complete with a picnic site, an eco-toilet and plenty of information. Interesting features just off the course of the Great Glen Way include Loch Laide and the Caiplich Prehistoric Settlement. Visitors can become Friends of the Abriachan Forest Trust, and receive a newsletter keeping them in touch with developments. Pick up a leaflet in the forest or check the website **www.abriachan.org.uk** for full contact details.

The Great Glen Way is waymarked as usual, but signposts also point back to Inverness and ahead to Drumnadrochit. The track is still part of the old drove road that was followed earlier, and it leads straight up along a broad forest ride. Swing left to pass a building near **Achpopuli** and climb fairly steeply, levelling out on a high point around 380m (1245ft). The track meanders gently downhill and leaves the forest at a gateway.

Continue to descend a moorland slope dotted with birch trees. There are boggy hollows spiked with rushes, as well as heathery humps, and a view of isolated buildings at **Corryfoyness**. Go through a tall gate into another forest, following a track that gradually moves closer towards Loch Ness. The first views over the loch are not particularly good, as the track descends gradually on a clear-felled slope. Views are lost as the track undulates, then suddenly gives way to a forest path.

The path runs downhill a short way, then crosses stepping stones over a small burn. Continue uphill, then downhill, then keep more or less level for a while. After passing through a more open area of grass and bracken, with birch trees, the path turns sharply left and right

A footbridge is crossed in a densely planted forest on the way from Corryfoyness to Drumnadrochit

downhill. The path enters dense forest with no views; little light reaches the forest floor, so only moss and wood sorrel grow alongside. Descend gradually to cross a footbridge, gaining a glimpse of Loch Ness before the path reaches a gate at the edge of the forest.

Follow the path across a grassy slope overlooking a stretch of **Loch Ness**, now featuring a view of **Urquhart Castle**. The path climbs through small gates, then enters woods and crosses a narrow access road that leads to Tychat. The path drops through more small gates and runs parallel to the main A82 road. There is another brief glimpse of Urquhart Castle across Urquhart Bay on Loch

Ness. Follow a path around a tall fence to pass **Temple House**, then go down through a gate and follow the access road down to the main road. There is access on the other side of the road for **Urquhart Bay** harbour, for cruises on Loch Ness.

> **John Cobb** broke land and water speed records. In 1947 his land speed record stood a little short of 400mph (645kph). On 29 September 1952 he achieved a speed of 206mph (331kph) on Loch Ness, from Urquhart Bay. Unfortunately, his craft *Crusader* disintegrated and sank, taking Cobb's life, and the engine wasn't recovered for 50 years.

Turn right to follow the main road, keeping to the pavement on the right-hand side throughout, passing a handful of B&Bs to reach **Drumnadrochit**.

LOCH NESS

Loch Ness occupies a deep trough that has been filled with water ever since the end of the Ice Age, around 10,000 years ago, and it reflects enough light to brighten even the dullest days in the Great Glen. Six major rivers carry water into Loch Ness, from a part of the Highlands known for high rainfall, explaining why the River Ness flows so powerfully past Inverness. Here are some facts and figures to help appreciate its full extent:

- Catchment area: 1800 sq km (700 square miles)
- Surface area: 56 sq km (21½ square miles)
- Length: 37km (23 miles)
- Width: 3km (2 miles)
- Shoreline length: 86km (53½ miles)
- Volume: 7.5 cu kilometres (1.8 cubic miles)
- Maximum depth: 230m (755ft)
- Surface level: 16m (52ft) above sea level

More astonishing facts include oft-repeated statements that the volume of water in the loch exceeds that of all the lakes and reservoirs in England and Wales, and is sufficient to immerse the entire population of the world!

Drumnadrochit (Gaelic – *Druim na Drochaid*) is a busy little village with plenty to catch the attention of passing tourists. Two attractions vying for attention are Nessieland, beside the Loch Ness Hotel, open all year (01456 450342, **www.nessieland.co.uk**), and the Loch Ness Centre & Exhibition at the Drumnadrochit Hotel, open all year (01456 450573, **www.lochness.com**). There are entrance charges to both places. Whatever you want to know about Loch Ness and its 'monster', this is the place to take on board all the opinions, then you can make up your own mind. If nothing more than a 'Nessie' souvenir is required, a handful of gift shops around the village deal in the widest selection of products.

There is accommodation to suit every pocket, from hotels to guest houses and B&Bs, with an independent hostel in Lewiston and a campsite further along the road at Borlum. Most facilities are clustered round the village green at Drumnadrochit. There is a bank with an ATM, a post office store, toilets, bars, restaurants, cafés and take-aways. There are souvenir and gift shops, as well as a tourist information centre (01456 459086). Regular daily Scottish Citylink buses link Drumnadrochit with Inverness and Fort William. Cruises on Loch Ness are also available (www.lochness-cruises.com).

STAGE 2A

Drumnadrochit to Invermoriston (high-level)

Start	Tourist Information Centre, Drumnadrochit (NH 507 299)
Finish	Glenmoriston Arms Hotel, Invermoriston (NH 420 168)
Distance	22.5km (14 miles)
Total ascent	580m (1900ft)
Time	5hr 45min
Terrain	Ascent to a moorland road. Forest tracks and upland moorland paths with some short, steep slopes.
Maps	OS Landrangers 26 and 34, OS Explorer 416S, Harvey Great Glen Way
Refreshments	Tearoom at a pottery at Grotaig. Invermoriston has a hotel with a bar/restaurant and one other restaurant.
Public Transport	Regular daily Scottish Citylink buses link Invermoriston and Drumnadrochit with Inverness and Fort William. Schooldays-only buses link Drumnadrochit and Grotaig.

On leaving Drumnadrochit, walkers have to decide whether to make a detour to visit Urquhart Castle, or console themselves by studying a floral model of the castle on the village green. There are two options for linking Drumnadrochit and Invermoriston, but a decision doesn't need to be made until halfway through the day. The high-level option should be open at all times, but in really bad weather it might be wise to take the low-level route (Stage 2B). Bear in mind that a pottery at Grotaig offers a tearoom, but otherwise there are no refreshments until Invermoriston is reached at the end of the day. The highest point on the Great Glen Way is reached on the slopes of Creag Dhearg. Later, there is an option to switch to the low-level route by walking down a forest track to Alltsigh. Despite the route running high and being just outside the forest, there are no views of Loch Ness towards the finish because the hills of Meall na Sròine and Creag nan Eun are in the way.

Invermoriston is a tiny village, which can be explored easily in the evening. It is wise to book lodgings in advance, although it is a simple matter to catch a bus elsewhere in search of accommodation.

For 1:25K route map see booklet pages 26–32.

Alternatively follow the path beside the main road, straight ahead to visit Urquhart Castle, then return to this junction later.

Follow the busy A82 road out of **Drumnadrochit**. The road bends right, then left to reach the neighbouring village of **Lewiston**, which has a small range of facilities. Cross the River Coiltie and turn right at a picnic area, as signposted for the Clunebeg Estate. ◀

Follow the minor road straight ahead to reach a big sign for the Clunebeg Estate, and continue walking along a clear track. Although the track runs level alongside the bouldery River Coiltie, densely packed trees usually screen the river from view. Any houses seen on the far side are part of the village of Lewiston. Admire tall

URQUHART CASTLE

Urquhart Castle is 2km (1¼ miles) off-route, or 3.25km (2 miles) from Drumnadrochit, perched on Strone Point overlooking Loch Ness. It can be reached safely on foot as there is a path beside the busy A82 road, and Scottish Citylink buses serve both Drumnadrochit and the castle. The situation is splendid and it is a renowned place for those keeping a lookout for the Loch Ness Monster! Once one of the largest castles in Scotland, Urquhart Castle's sprawling ruins take time to explore. A visitor centre offers a thorough grounding in its construction and history, plus a café. Urquhart Castle is open all year, and there is an entrance charge (01456 450551).

A Bronze Age promontory fort once stood on Strone Point, and there were other defensive structures on the site before Urquhart Castle was built in the 13th century. Its history is one of intense conflict, in which English and Scots alternately occupied it, with William Wallace and Robert the Bruce each holding the property for a time. Buchan, son of Robert II, held the castle from 1390, ruling with brutal force, and frequently robbing churches. In the 15th and 16th centuries the MacDonalds launched raids on the castle, which was later held by the Grants. The bulk of the damage to the castle was done with explosives in 1692, which prevented it becoming a Jacobite stronghold in subsequent years.

Visitors cross a wooden gangway across a defensive ditch, and pass through a gatehouse. However, in the past, most people approaching the castle would have done so through a watergate from Loch Ness. The centrepiece of the Urquhart Castle is a stout and impressive tower house, but be sure to take note of the complex arrangement of the ruined defensive walls that surround the site. The best vantage point is of course from the top of the tower house.

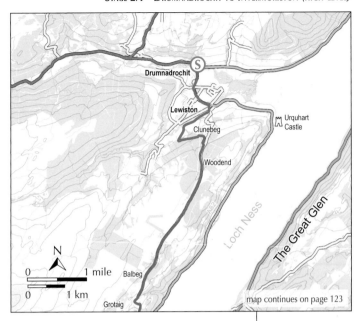

Drumnadrochit

Lewiston

Clunebeg

Urquhart Castle

Woodend

Loch Ness

The Great Glen

N

0   1 mile   Balbeg

0   1 km

Grotaig

map continues on page 123

oaks and beech trees alongside the track up to Clunebeg House then follow a waymarked path straight ahead from **Clunebeg Lodge**, restaurant and B&B. The path swings left as it climbs across a slope of fine oaks and bracken, and there are views back towards Drumnadrochit. Go through a gate and cross a footbridge into dense forest, where there is later a brief glimpse of Drumnadrochit to the left. The path turns right and runs up to a gate on a track, where a left turn leads quickly up to another gate and a minor road.

Turn right as signposted for the Great Glen Way, climbing steeply up past a house called **Woodend**. The road climbs at a gentler gradient and later leaves the forest. A path runs parallel, off to the right, as the road undulates across heather moorland around 250m (820ft). The road has to be followed again, between swathes of rough grassland and improved pasture. Gorse flanks the road

The route follows a path from Grotaig, high above Ruskich Wood

Keeping straight ahead leads, in less than 200 metres, to the Loch Ness Clay Works pottery and tearoom at Grotaig.

as it descends a boggy moorland slope, later passing the Ancarraig lodges access. Use another path running parallel to the road, and look ahead to see the humped hills of Meall Fuar-mhonaidh and Creag Dhearg. There are occasional glimpses of Loch Ness while passing isolated houses and farms on the way to **Balbeg**, finally dropping to a car park, then watch for the Great Glen Way turning left through a gate. ◄

Walk down a track and cross a concrete bridge over Grotaig Burn. The track runs through a field, passing through patchy woodlands, then below a fort on the little hill of Dùn Scriben. Enter forest and follow a convoluted path through gates while running parallel to a track.

The path climbs away from the track and there are occasional views of Loch Ness. Pass a log bench and note how the forest edges are often softened by birch. The path joins a track in the forest above **Ruskich Wood**. Follow the track past **Lòn na Fola** and later cross a bridge over a waterfall. Keep walking to reach a junction of tracks, where the high-level and low-level routes part. Keep right (the low-level route – Stage 2B – turns sharp left downhill).

The track rises across a clear-felled and replanted slope, where occasional Scots pines have been left standing tall, among abundant rosebay willowherb. The track reaches a stone-built windbreak, where views across Loch Ness feature the remote Monadh Liath range rolling southwards into the distance. Turn right before reaching the windbreak to follow a waymarked path up the forested slope. The path climbs steeply at times and crosses a rock step.

The path rises from the forest and easily traverses the rugged slopes of **Creag Dhearg**. The highest point on the Great Glen Way is reached, around 415m (1360ft), and another stone-built windbreak is passed, with a fine view of Loch Ness. The path winds downhill and

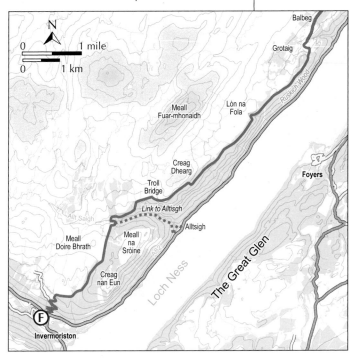

The track can be followed straight ahead and downhill for 2km (1¼ miles), reaching the low-level route at Alltsigh, close to Briarbank B&B, Loch Ness Youth Hostel and bus services.

features a few stone steps at one point. The rustic **Troll Bridge** is crossed, perched above a waterfall. Cross another footbridge later, while following the path just outside the forest, beside a tall deer fence.

Wind further downhill, back into the forest to join a track. Follow the track, which later swings left over a concrete bridge spanning **Allt Saigh**. ◀ Turn right as marked up a clear path, later passing a couple of stone slabs that flank the path like old gateposts. Pass the little hill of **Meall Doire Bhrath**, around 330m (1080ft), and note a curious sculpture on the right, where tree branches have been woven into a circle, mounted on a stone plinth.

THE SEVEN MEN OF GLEN MORISTON

The date was 27 July 1746, when Bonnie Prince Charlie was on the run after the crushing defeat at the Battle of Culloden. Pursued by 'Butcher' Cumberland, and with a bounty of £30,000 on his head, Charles had not eaten for two days and was clad in rags by the time he reached Glen Moriston. Coming upon a crude hut and ravenously hungry, he was warned by his companions not to seek food or shelter in case he was recognised. Charles declared 'I had better be killed like a man than starved like a fool', and made his way to the hut. The seven men inside were mere outlaws, and one of them recognised him, but to their credit, they spurned the chance to claim the bounty and risked their lives to feed and shelter him. Meanwhile, on the road through Glen Moriston, an Edinburgh merchant named Roderick MacKenzie, who bore a passing resemblance to the Bonnie Prince, was shot at by troops. As he died he declared, 'Alas, you have killed your prince', and this ruse was sufficient to buy enough time for Charles to be smuggled out of the country.

Invermoriston (Gaelic – *Inbhir Mor Eason*) has only a few facilities, but at the end of the day these prove most welcome. The Glenmoriston Arms Hotel is very prominent. It was originally a drovers' inn, dating from 1740, and the oldest parts are around the bar and reception area. Johnson and Boswell stayed there while planning a trip to the Hebrides in 1773. There are a few B&Bs in and around the village, as well as the Glenmoriston Stores Post Office, the Clog and Craft Shop, and further along the Skye Road, the Glen Rowan Coffee Shop and Restaurant. Toilets are available inside the Glenmoriston Millennium Hall, when open. Regular daily Scottish Citylink buses link Invermoriston with Inverness and Fort William, as well as the Isle of Skye.

The path reaches a turning space at the end of a track. Follow the track straight ahead, through partly clear-felled forest. Later, turn right down another path and cross a footbridge over a stream. The path winds uphill, with stone steps where it gets steeper. Old birch trees are dotted around on the slopes outside the forest. When the path descends, it follows a drystone wall, with the forest left and a field right. When the lower corner of the wall is reached, turn left through the forest to reach a track. The high-level route re-joins the low-level route at this point. ▸

Turn right to follow the track, crossing a bridge over a stream to join a road. Turn sharp left down the road and cross another bridge over the same stream. Densely planted conifers are passed on the descent, giving way to birch, oak, beech and sycamore, with a holly understorey. The steep and narrow road zigzags past Craik na Dav B&B, reaching a junction with the A887. Turn left to pass the Clog and Craft Shop, where a milestone warns 'Last Clog Shop before Skye – 52 miles'. The little village of **Invermoriston** lies directly ahead.

The high-level route descends through forest and woods above Invermoriston

Just across the track, a steep and winding gravel path offers a short-cut down to a road.

STAGE 2B

Drumnadrochit to Invermoriston (low-level)

Start	Tourist Information Centre, Drumnadrochit (NH 507 299)
Finish	Glenmoriston Arms Hotel, Invermoriston (NH 420 168)
Distance	23.5km (14½ miles)
Total ascent	590m (1935ft)
Time	5hr 30min
Terrain	Ascent to a moorland road. Forest tracks and paths with some short, steep slopes.
Maps	OS Landrangers 26 and 34, OS Explorer 416S, Harvey Great Glen Way
Refreshments	Tearoom at a pottery at Grotaig. Snacks at Briarbank B&B at Alltsigh. Invermoriston has a hotel with a bar/restaurant and one other restaurant.
Public Transport	Regular daily Scottish Citylink buses link Invermoriston and Drumnadrochit with Inverness and Fort William. Schooldays-only buses link Drumnadrochit and Grotaig.

On leaving Drumnadrochit, walkers have to decide whether to make a detour to visit Urquhart Castle, or console themselves by studying a floral model of the castle on the village green. There are two options for linking Drumnadrochit and Invermoriston, but a decision doesn't need to be made until halfway through the day. Before making firm plans to follow the low-level route please note that it might sometimes be closed for timber harvesting. Check in advance on the Great Glen Way website, and if the route is closed switch to the high-level option (Stage 2A). The low-level route is easier, but it is also slightly longer.

Most of the day's walk is spent close to Loch Ness, with only occasional views, but this will change as more and more areas are clear-felled. Later, there is an option to switch to the high-level route by walking up a forest track from Alltsigh, otherwise stay on the low-level route all the way to Invermoriston.

For 1:25K route map see booklet pages 26–32.

Follow the busy A82 road out of **Drumnadrochit**. The road bends right, then left to reach the neighbouring village of **Lewiston**, which has a small range of facilities.

Cross the River Coiltie and turn right at a picnic area, as signposted for the Clunebeg Estate. ▶

Alternatively follow the path beside the main road, straight ahead to visit Urquhart Castle, then return to this junction later.

Urquhart Castle is 2km (1¼ miles) off-route, or 3.25km (2 miles) from Drumnadrochit, perched on Strone Point overlooking Loch Ness. It can be reached safely on foot as there is a path beside the busy A82 road, and Scottish Citylink buses serve both Drumnadrochit and the castle. The situation is splendid and it is a renowned place for those keeping a lookout for the Loch Ness 'monster'! Once one of the largest castles in Scotland, Urquhart Castle's sprawling ruins take time to explore. A visitor centre offers a thorough grounding in its construction and history, plus a café. Urquhart Castle is open all year, and there is an entrance charge (01456 450551). For more information see Stage 2B.

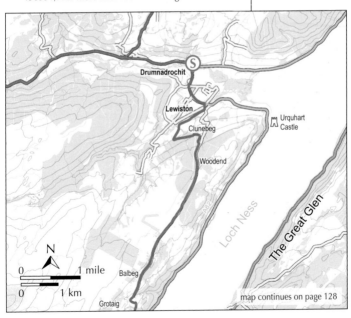

map continues on page 128

Follow the minor road straight ahead to reach a big sign for the Clunebeg Estate, and continue walking along a clear track. Although the track runs level alongside the bouldery River Coiltie, densely packed trees usually screen the river from view. Any houses seen on the far side are part of the village of Lewiston. Admire tall oaks and beech trees while following the track up to Clunebeg House and follow a waymarked path straight ahead from **Clunebeg Lodge**, restaurant and B&B. The path swings left as it climbs across a slope of fine oaks and bracken, and there are views back towards Drumnadrochit. Go through a gate and cross a footbridge to enter dense forest, with a brief glimpse of Drumnadrochit to the left later. The path turns right and runs up to a gate on a track,

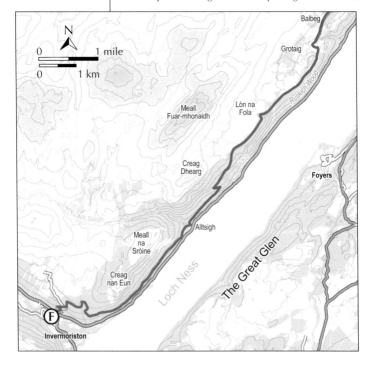

where a left turn leads quickly up to another gate and a minor road.

Turn right as signposted for the Great Glen Way, climbing steeply up past a house called **Woodend**. The road ascends more gently and later leaves the forest. A path runs parallel, to the right, as the road undulates across heather moorland around 250m (820ft). The road has to be followed again, between swathes of rough grassland and improved pasture. Gorse flanks the road as it descends a boggy moorland slope, later passing the Ancarraig lodges access. Use another path running parallel, and look ahead to see the humped hills of Meall Fuar-mhonaidh and Creag Dhearg. There are occasional glimpses of Loch Ness while passing isolated houses and farms on the way to **Balbeg**, finally dropping to a car park, then watch for the Great Glen Way turning left through a gate. ▶

Walk down a track and cross a concrete bridge over Grotaig Burn. The track runs through a field, passing through patchy woodlands, then below a fort on the little hill of Dùn Scriben. Enter forest and follow a convoluted path through gates, parallel to a track.

The path climbs away from the track and there are occasional views of Loch Ness. Pass a log bench and note how the forest edges are often softened by birch. The path joins a track in the forest above **Ruskich Wood**. Follow the track past **Lòn na Fola** and later cross a bridge over a waterfall. Keep walking to reach a junction of tracks, where the low-level and high-level routes part. Turn sharp left downhill (the high-level route – Stage 2A – keeps right).

The track descends and later makes a sharp right turn, descending further. Later, the track bends quickly left and right as it continues its descent. Another sharp left and right turn are made, while views through the Great Glen are lost as the track passes tall conifers. Simply keep walking downhill to reach a track junction at **Alltsigh**.

Before reaching the junction, note a short-cut on the left to Briarbank B&B (which also offers snacks and drinks). At the junction, turning left leads

Walking straight ahead leads, in less than 200 metres, to the Loch Ness Clay Works pottery and tearoom at Grotaig.

A view of Loch Ness from the rugged garden in front of Loch Ness Youth Hostel at Alltsigh

quickly to the busy A82 road beside Loch Ness, where turning left again leads to **Loch Ness Youth Hostel** and a bus stop. The hostel has splendid views across the loch.

Those who don't need to detour to Alltsigh can keep straight along a forest track as marked, crossing a concrete bridge over a rocky gorge with a waterfall and beautiful trees. A diligent search will reveal an old pack-horse bridge. Climb steeply, passing a track junction, then follow an undulating track fringed with broom. Keep straight ahead at a track junction beside a rock cutting, climbing gently for a while and passing a slope of gorse bushes. A bend is reached where there is a good view-point revealing the length of Loch Ness, but also turn and admire the fine variety of trees stacked against the cliffs of **Creag nan Eun**. Later, while climbing uphill, a post draws attention to the 'Stone Cave', said to have been built to offer shelter to a washerwoman on her frequent journeys between Alltsigh and Invermoriston. It still offers splendid shelter. Continue uphill at a gentle gradient, with occasional glimpses of Loch Ness, then turn right to ascend a narrow and bendy forest path as marked, to reach another forest track.

Turn left to follow the track, then left at a nearby junction as marked, but also consider turning right to see a signpost for a viewpoint. This short detour reveals a narrow path winding up a slope covered in ling and bell heather to reach the crude 'Stone Seat' where there is a fine view over **Loch Ness**. The village of Invermoriston, despite being close to hand, is completely hidden from view. Retrace steps to the junction. Follow the track uphill to another junction, then turn left and go through a tall gateway. Follow the track across a concrete bridge over a stream. The track swings left, then right, then while crossing a crest, a thinner part of the plantation reveals some of the former heather cover and low rocky outcrops. The

One of several vigorous streams crossed by the trail

A steep and winding gravel path on the left offers a short-cut down to a road.

track makes a gentle descent among closely packed trees. The high-level route re-joins the low-level. ◄

Follow the track onwards, crossing a bridge over a stream to join a road. Turn sharp left down the road and cross another bridge over the same stream. Densely planted conifers are passed on the descent, giving way to birch, oak, beech and sycamore, with a holly understorey. The steep and narrow road zigzags past Craik na Dav B&B, reaching a junction with the A887 road. Turn left to pass the Clog and Craft Shop, where a milestone warns 'Last Clog Shop before Skye – 52 miles'. The little village of **Invermoriston** lies directly ahead.

THE SEVEN MEN OF GLEN MORISTON

The date was 27 July 1746, when Bonnie Prince Charlie was on the run after the crushing defeat at the Battle of Culloden. Pursued by 'Butcher' Cumberland, and with a bounty of £30,000 on his head, Charles had not eaten for two days and was clad in rags by the time he reached Glen Moriston. Coming upon a crude hut and ravenously hungry, he was warned by his companions not to seek food or shelter in case he was recognised. Charles declared 'I had better be killed like a man than starved like a fool', and made his way to the hut. The seven men inside were mere outlaws, and one of them recognised him, but to their credit, they spurned the chance to claim the bounty and risked their lives to feed and shelter him. Meanwhile, on the road through Glen Moriston, an Edinburgh merchant named Roderick MacKenzie, who bore a passing resemblance to the Bonnie Prince, was shot at by troops. As he died he declared, 'Alas, you have killed your prince', and this ruse was sufficient to buy enough time for Charles to be smuggled out of the country.

Invermoriston (Gaelic – *Inbhir Mor Eason*) has only a few facilities, but at the end of the day these prove most welcome. The Glenmoriston Arms Hotel is very prominent. It was originally a drovers' inn, dating from 1740, and the oldest parts are around the bar and reception area. Johnson and Boswell stayed there while planning a trip to the Hebrides in 1773. There are a few B&Bs in and around the village, as well as the Glenmoriston Stores Post Office, the Clog and Craft Shop, and further along the Skye Road, the Glen Rowan Coffee Shop and Restaurant. Toilets are available inside the Glenmoriston Millennium Hall, when open. Regular daily Scottish Citylink buses link Invermoriston with Inverness and Fort William, as well as the Isle of Skye.

STAGE 3A

Invermoriston to Fort Augustus (high-level)

Start	Glenmoriston Arms Hotel, Invermoriston (NH 420 168)
Finish	Fort Augustus Tourist Information Centre (NH 378 094)
Distance	12km (7½ miles)
Total ascent	710m (2330ft)
Time	3hr 15min
Terrain	Forest tracks and upland moorland paths with some short, steep slopes.
Maps	OS Landranger 34, OS Explorer 416S, Harvey Great Glen Way
Refreshments	Plenty of bars, restaurants, cafés and take-aways around Fort Augustus.
Public Transport	Regular daily Scottish Citylink buses link Invermoriston and Fort Augustus with Inverness and Fort William.

There are two options for linking Invermoriston with Fort Augustus. The high-level option should be open at all times, but in really bad weather it might be wise to take the low-level option (Stage 3B). In good weather it isn't particularly difficult, and some walkers might add it to the following day's walk (Stage 4) if they are trying to cover the Great Glen Way in a hurry. Alternatively, the afternoon could be spent exploring Fort Augustus, or taking a short cruise on Loch Ness in order to gain a greater appreciation of its vastness.

The high-level route of the Great Glen Way climbs above the forested northern slopes of Loch Ness, allowing much more wide-ranging views than are gained from the low-level option.

Leave **Invermoriston** by following the main A82 road downhill to cross the River Moriston, then turn right along a minor road. However, note the ravaged remains of Telford's Bridge spanning the river, and the splendid Moriston Falls that spill beneath it.

For 1:25K route map see booklet pages 22–26.

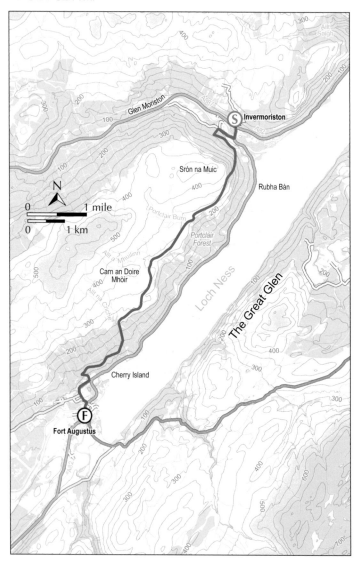

The ramshackle remains of **Telford's Bridge**, also known as the Old Bridge, could be crossed in preference to the main road bridge, but take care as the masonry is in a bad state of repair. Despite being nothing more than a standard double-span stone arch, its construction spanned several years from 1805 until 1813, owing to a 'languid and inattentive contractor' and 'idle workers'. The bridge is one of more than a thousand associated with Telford.

The minor road leads to Dalcataig, but the Great Glen Way suddenly turns left up a winding path on a clear-felled slope. Just before reaching a forest track, turn left as marked along an older track running parallel. Pass big beech trees, birch and alder, rather than conifers. The old track and the forest track join later. The high-level route turns right up a path (the low-level route – Stage 3B – runs straight ahead along the forest track).

The path climbs, quickly crossing another forest track, becoming steeper as it winds up the forested slope,

A path climbs a clear-felled slope from Glen Moriston

135

occasionally featuring stone steps. Emerge from the forest below the rugged face of **Sròn na Muic**. The path traverses the slope above the forest, passing a stone bench and later crossing a couple of footbridges. Briefly touch the edge of the forest, descend to pass beneath a power line, and cross another footbridge. The path surface is firm, with good drainage, while the moorland supports grass, heather and bog myrtle.

Cross another two footbridges close together, where there are waterfalls on **Portclair Burn**. Continue traversing across the rugged moorland slopes above the forest, crossing a couple more footbridges. Descend into a valley to cross a footbridge over the **Allt a' Mhuilinn**. The path winds as it climbs from the valley, reaching a stone-built windbreak shelter on a shoulder of **Carn an Doire Mhòir**, around 315m (1035ft), where there are fine views of Loch Ness.

The path continues with good views, winding and undulating, with a few stone steps leading up and down. Pass another viewpoint around 225m (740ft), then follow the path downhill as it eventually drops into the forest. There are vigorous little waterfalls alongside as the path

From the high-level route there are views across Loch Ness to Beinn a' Bhacaidh

winds down to a forest track. Turn right and cross a bridge over a waterfall on the **Allt na Criche**, then turn left down another path, passing more waterfalls.

The path reaches a junction with a forest track on the Allt na Criche Trail. Turn right to follow the track gently downhill, reaching a junction where the high-level route and low-level route re-join. Keep right to follow the forest track uphill, pausing at a noticeboard overlooking the head of **Loch Ness**, above **Cherry Island**.

> There is only one island in Loch Ness; the diminutive **Cherry Island** near Fort Augustus, which is actually an ancient man-made island dwelling, or *crannog*.

Continue up the track and cross a bridge. Later, turn left down a path on a steep slope covered in tall, stately pines. Cross a footbridge at the foot of the slope to reach a road at Three Bridges. Turn right and follow the narrow road past a few B&Bs, reaching a junction. ▸

Follow the road straight ahead, which is Bunoich Brae, passing Morag's Lodge Independent Hostel. Turn right down a tarmac path, short-cutting past a nearby road junction. Turn right to follow the busy A82, reaching the tourist information centre in **Fort Augustus**.

A right turn at the junction, for Jenkins Park and Auchterawe, leads to the Great Glen Way Rangers' base.

FORT AUGUSTUS

The earliest settlement at Fort Augustus (Gaelic – *Cill Chuimein*) was founded in the 6th century by monks from Iona, led by St Cumin. Precious little else is recorded about the place until, in the aftermath of the Jacobite Rising of 1715, a fort was constructed on the site now occupied by the Lovat Hotel. When General Wade built a military road through the area in 1726, the fort was moved to where the Abbey now stands. Fort Augustus was named after William Augustus, Duke of Cumberland, and was destroyed at the beginning of the Jacobite Rising of 1745. 'Butcher' Cumberland had it rebuilt while engaged in a brutal campaign to suppress the Highland clans. In 1876 the site was given to the Benedictines who built the Abbey, vacating it in 1997. The Abbey has since been redeveloped and there is no longer any public access.

The bustling tourist village of Fort Augustus is halfway along the Great Glen Way. It offers plenty of accommodation, from a campsite, hostels and humble B&Bs to fine hotels. There is a bank, and an ATM at the Spar shop. There is a post office and a choice of food and gift shops, several bars, restaurants, cafés and take-aways. Toilets are located beside the tourist information centre (0845 2255121). There are regular daily bus services to Fort William and Inverness. A variety of cruises on Loch Ness are also available. An interesting rural attraction close to the village is the Highland and Rare Breeds Park, signposted from the bridge, open all year, with an entrance charge, or honesty box when unstaffed (01320 366433).

The Caledonian Canal Visitor Centre beside the canal

STAGE 3B

Invermoriston to Fort Augustus (low-level)

Start	Glenmoriston Arms Hotel, Invermoriston (NH 420 168)
Finish	Fort Augustus Tourist Information Centre (NH 378 094)
Distance	12km (7½ miles)
Total ascent	320m (1050ft)
Time	3hr
Terrain	Forest tracks and paths with some short, steep slopes.
Maps	OS Landranger 34, OS Explorer 416S, Harvey Great Glen Way
Refreshments	Plenty of bars, restaurants, cafés and take-aways around Fort Augustus.
Public Transport	Regular daily Scottish Citylink buses link Invermoriston and Fort Augustus with Inverness and Fort William.

There are two options for linking Invermoriston with Fort Augustus. Before making firm plans to follow the low-level option, please note that it might sometimes be closed for timber harvesting. Check in advance on the Great Glen Way website, and if the route is closed, then switch to the high-level option (Stage 3A). This is a short day, and some walkers might add it to the previous day's walk (Stage 2) if they are trying to cover the Great Glen Way in a hurry. Alternatively, the afternoon could be spent exploring Fort Augustus, or taking a short cruise on Loch Ness in order to gain a greater appreciation of its vastness.

The low-level route of the Great Glen Way often runs close to Loch Ness, but the forested slopes usually shield it from view, so walkers see less of it than they might imagine.

Leave **Invermoriston** by following the main A82 road downhill to cross the River Moriston, then turn right along a minor road. However, note the ravaged remains of Telford's Bridge spanning the river, and the splendid Moriston Falls that spill beneath it.

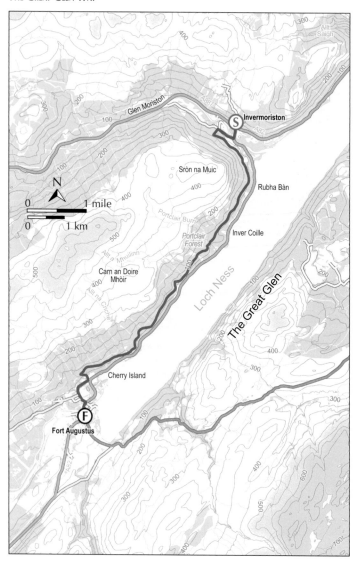

The ramshackle remains of **Telford's Bridge**, also known as the Old Bridge, could be crossed in preference to the main road bridge, but take care as the masonry is in a bad state of repair. Despite being nothing more than a standard double-span stone arch, its construction spanned several years from 1805 until 1813, owing to a 'languid and inattentive contractor' and 'idle workers'. The bridge is one of more than a thousand associated with Telford.

The Glenmoriston Arms Hotel was a drover's inn, dating from 1740

The minor road leads to Dalcataig, but the Great Glen Way suddenly turns left up a winding path on a clear-felled slope. Just before reaching a forest track, turn left as marked along an older track running parallel. Pass big beech trees, birch and alder, rather than conifers. The old track and the forest track join later. The low-level route continues straight ahead, past a track junction (the high-level route – Stage 3A – turns right).

The track enjoys a brief view of Loch Ness as it swings right to leave **Glen Moriston**, crossing a crest and running downhill. A broader track is reached at a junction, so keep right, in effect straight ahead, to climb steeply.

The River Moriston and Falls of Moriston can be explored from Invermoriston

A campsite at Inver Coille is marked off-route, down to the left.

The gradient eases and there are eventually good views of Loch Ness from a clear-felled slope. A gentle descent leads across a concrete bridge over a small waterfall, losing the views and crossing a dip in the track. ◄ Cross a concrete bridge over **Portclair Burn**, climb gently, then there are more views across Loch Ness, taking in the hill of Beinn a' Bhacaidh rising from the far shore. Descend gently into tall forest, where a concrete bridge spans a waterfall on the **Allt a' Mhullinn**. The track climbs over a gentle rise where there is a stone-slab seat; views both ways along Loch Ness seem endless, as well as stretching across the loch to the rugged hill of Beinn a' Bhacaidh.

Follow the undulating track, enjoying good views over a slope of young trees. Descend gradually among tall trees and keep straight ahead at a junction. There is a slight dip in the track, then a descent among tall conifers, with margins of heather, bilberry, mosses, ferns and wood sorrel. Pass a gate and avoid a right turn as the track descends and bends. The lower woods are mixed, with some fine oaks and birch, then the track swings left to cross a tumbling stream at **Allt na Criche**, almost reaching the busy main road.

Just before the road turn right through a gate and follow another track uphill. Plenty of birch trees grow among the conifers, and a junction is reached where the low-level and high-level routes re-join. Walk straight ahead to follow the forest track uphill, pausing at a noticeboard overlooking the head of **Loch Ness**, above **Cherry Island**.

> There is only one island in Loch Ness; the diminutive **Cherry Island** near Fort Augustus, which is actually an ancient man-made island dwelling, or *crannog*.

Continue up the track and cross a bridge. Later, turn left down a path on a steep slope covered in tall, stately pines. Cross a footbridge at the bottom to reach a road at Three Bridges. Turn right and follow the narrow road past a few B&Bs, reaching a junction. ▸

Follow the road straight ahead, which is Bunoich Brae, passing Morag's Lodge Independent Hostel. Turn right down a tarmac path, short-cutting past a nearby road junction. Turn right to follow the busy A82, reaching the tourist information centre in **Fort Augustus**.

A right turn at the junction, for Jenkins Park and Auchterawe, leads to the Great Glen Way Rangers' base.

A footbridge spans a stream near the first houses at Fort Augustus

FORT AUGUSTUS

The earliest settlement at Fort Augustus (Gaelic – *Cill Chuimein*) was founded in the 6th century by monks from Iona, led by St Cumin. Precious little else is recorded about the place until, in the aftermath of the Jacobite Rising of 1715, a fort was constructed on the site now occupied by the Lovat Hotel. When General Wade built a military road through the area in 1726, the fort was moved to where the Abbey now stands. For more information see Stage 3A.

The bustling tourist village of Fort Augustus is halfway along the Great Glen Way. It offers plenty of accommodation, from a campsite, hostels and humble B&Bs to fine hotels. There is a bank, and an ATM at the Spar shop. There is a post office and a choice of food and gift shops, several bars, restaurants, cafés and take-aways. Toilets are located beside the tourist information centre (0845 2255121). The Great Glen Rangers have an office in the forest at Auchtertawe, not far from Fort Augustus (see Appendix A). There are regular daily bus services to Fort William and Inverness. A variety of cruises on Loch Ness are also available. An interesting rural attraction close to the village is the Highland and Rare Breeds Croft, signposted from the bridge, open all year, with an entrance charge, or honesty box when unstaffed (01320 366433).

A flight of five canal locks cuts the village of Fort Augustus in two, and proves immensely popular with visitors

STAGE 4

Fort Augustus to Laggan Locks

Start	Fort Augustus Tourist Information Centre (NH 378 094)
Finish	Laggan Locks (NN 286 963)
Distance	17.5km (10¾ miles)
Total ascent	40m (130ft)
Time	4hr 30min
Terrain	A clear and firm canal-side track leads to Aberchalder. Tracks and paths beside Loch Oich can be wet and muddy.
Maps	OS Landranger 34, OS Explorer 400, Harvey Great Glen Way
Refreshments	Tea garden at Aberchalder Swing Bridge. Restaurant and bar at the Great Glen Water Park.
Public Transport	Regular daily Scottish Citylink buses link Fort Augustus and Laggan with Inverness and Fort William.

This is a splendid day's walk, where the walls of the Great Glen rise closer to hand and there are often views of the high mountains further beyond. The Great Glen Way climbs up a steep flight of five locks as it follows the Caledonian Canal away from Fort Augustus. A lovely stretch of the canal gradually rises to Aberchalder, where it is worth making a slight detour to admire the Bridge of Oich. The summit level of the canal is at Loch Oich, which is passed using a stretch of General Wade's military road, as well as part of an old railway line. Richly wooded slopes are protected as a nature reserve on the way to North Laggan, where facilities are very limited. A short stroll along the Caledonian Canal completes the day's walk.

Leave the tourist information centre in **Fort Augustus** by following the A82 road in the direction of Fort William. Cross a bridge over the River Oich to reach a swing bridge on the **Caledonian Canal**. Don't cross the swing bridge, but turn right and climb beside a flight of locks, passing the Caledonian Canal Visitor Centre.

For 1:25K route map see booklet pages 17–22.

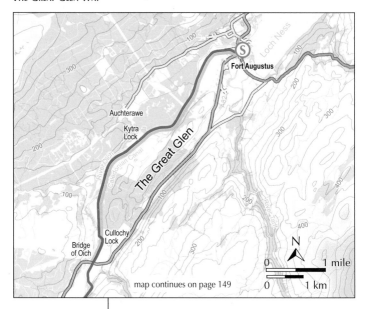

map continues on page 149

As walkers ascend the flight of five locks through Fort Augustus, metal disks along the way pose all sorts of questions about the Caledonian Canal, its history, construction and use. Visitors who want to find the answers are directed to the **Caledonian Canal Visitor Centre**, just across the road. A small exhibition space can be explored, there are books on sale about the canal, while British Waterways Scotland staff are on hand to deal with any queries. The centre is open 10am–5.30pm, April to October, and entry is free (01320 366493).

After passing the top lock, the canal gradually bends to the left and views of Fort Augustus are lost. A covered overspill weir allows excess water to fall into the **River Oich**, and there are glimpses of the river from time to time, as both the canal and river run parallel. The canal passes a power line and bends gradually to the right.

A fine row of pine trees grows along the opposite bank. Hazel trees are abundant along the bank being followed, and tall pines flank the canal on both sides at **Kytra Lock**. ▸

After passing Kytra Lock an overspill weir has to be crossed, and this could mean wet feet if there is excess water in the canal, though this would be a very rare occurrence. The canal broadens considerably where a small loch was incorporated into its course. Later several particularly tall and graceful birch trees are passed. When **Cullochy Lock** is reached, cross over the lock gates to pick up and follow a track on the other side of the canal. Look across the water to spot a large overspill weir to the River Oich. A clear track runs beside the canal and passes the Bridge House Tea Garden to reach the **Aberchalder Swing Bridge** and A82. ▸

Cross the road and follow a path alongside the canal, then cross a ladder stile on the left to continue along the shore of **Loch Oich**. Go through a kissing gate and turn right to cross an old railway bridge over the Calder Burn. The Great Glen Way reaches a couple of gates on the Aberchalder Estate Road.

> **Loch Oich** is the smallest of the three lochs linked by the Caledonian Canal. It measures 6.5km (4 miles) in length and is only 0.5km (0.3 miles) across at its widest point. Loch Oich's greatest depth is 40.5m (133ft), but it had to be deepened at both ends to accommodate traffic using the Caledonian Canal. The surface level of the loch is 32m (105ft), which is also the summit level for the canal.

Turn right, away from the gates, to cross a bridge at a small waterfall. As the track, which is an old military road, runs gently uphill, watch out for a miniature iron aqueduct on the right, carrying water across the old railway line. Walk steeply down through a rocky, mossy cutting, crossing over an old railway tunnel, where both the track and old railway line have to avoid a cliff dropping sheer into the lake.

A basic 'Trailblazer Rest' campsite is available. A key for the toilet needs to be obtained in advance via the Great Glen Way website or Caledonian Canal office.

A couple of B&Bs can be found by following the main road in either direction, but they lie well off-route and traffic can be very busy. See the 'Invergarry Link' (Stages 4A/5A) for details of an alternative route.

The path alongside Loch Oich often runs across a well-wooded slope

A very basic 'Trailblazer Rest' campsite is available. A key for the toilet needs to be obtained in advance via the Great Glen Way website or Caledonian Canal office.

The track briefly touches the lake shore and continues through woods, then runs through a meadow and passes **Leitirfearn Cottage**. ◀ Watch out for a crenelated concrete arch on the left, which supports the old railway trackbed. The track proceeds along the shore of Loch Oich, with views across it from time to time when the trees thin out. The ruins of Invergarry Castle might be seen on the far shore. Go through a gate and climb uphill a short way to continue along the old railway trackbed. The surroundings are vividly green and are managed as a nature reserve.

Leitirfearn Forest Nature Reserve features a lush, damp, vibrantly green woodland: a mix of ash, birch, elm and hazel. The steep slopes support cushions of moss and delicate ferns, as well as flowers in

spring and fungi in autumn. It has the appearance
of a jungle, yet it has been cut back twice to accommodate a road and railway. General Wade pushed
a road through the woods around 1725, while the
Invergarry and Fort Augustus Railway Company
opened a line here in 1903. Both routes fell from
favour, the road switching to the other side of the
loch and the railway being abandoned in 1946.

The old trackbed features some cuttings and there
are later clumps of rhododendron before the route drifts
to the right and lands on a narrow tarmac road at the
Great Glen Water Park.

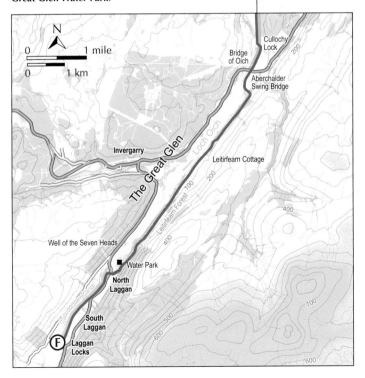

The **Invergarry and Fort Augustus Railway Museum** (**www.invergarrystation.org.uk**) is being developed adjacent to the water park. A section of railway track has been restored.

A sign points off-route for the Well of the Seven Heads Store. The shop is over 1 km (½ mile) away and the road to it can be very busy.

A right turn off-route leads in a few paces to a bar and restaurant surrounded by wooden chalets on the shores of Loch Oich. If a visit isn't required, then simply turn left and follow the quiet road to a junction with the busy A82 road. ◀

Cross over the road with care near the Laggan Swing Bridge. Follow a path through an area of bracken above the Caledonian Canal. Pass broom, gorse and brambles while passing high above a mooring stage, then cross a footbridge over a canal feeder, the Allt an Lagain. There is access on the left to the A82, not far from the Great Glen Hostel in **North Laggan**. Take care if following the road there.

Rhododendron and broom are common beside the canal. The path broadens to a grassy track and passes a slope of pine trees. Pass the *Eagle* barge and bar/restaurant, and follow the canal-side embankment, keeping left of a cottage to reach the double lock at **Laggan Locks**. Nearby facilities are very limited.

A conflict known as the '**Battle of the Shirts**' took place at Laggan in the 16th century. The seeds were sown, as was often the case among Highland clans, with a perceived insult. Ranald Galda, of Clanranald, had been reared among the Frasers, and when he returned to his home a feast was prepared by way of welcome. As seven oxen were slaughtered, Ranald remarked that a few hens would have been sufficient, thus spurning the hospitality of his hosts. They called him 'Ranald of the Hens' and said that he could return to the Frasers if he didn't like it.

It was an uncomfortably hot day in 1544 when 300 Frasers faced a combined force of 600 MacDonalds and Camerons to settle the score at Laggan. Both sides had to put aside their hot and heavy woollen plaids and fight each other wearing

long undershirts; hence the name 'Battle of the Shirts'. Neither side scored a victory, since the carnage was so great that only four Frasers and eight of their opponents were left standing at the conclusion of the battle.

Looking from Laggan Locks across Ceann Loch, flanked by the slopes of the Great Glen

LAGGAN

Laggan (Gaelic – *Lagan*) is a sprawling settlement with no clear centre. South Laggan is the area near Laggan Locks, while North Laggan is closer to the Laggan Swing Bridge, over 2km (1¼ miles) away. Facilities are limited to the Great Glen Hostel and a couple of B&B places. Basic camping is available near the locks. The *Eagle* is a converted Dutch barge that operates as a floating bar restaurant near Laggan Locks, and the next nearest restaurant is back at the Great Glen Water Park. Regular daily Scottish Citylink buses link Laggan with Fort William, Fort Augustus and Inverness.

STAGE 5
Laggan Locks to Gairlochy

Start	Laggan Locks (NN 286 963)
Finish	Gairlochy Bottom Lock (NN 176 842)
Distance	19km (12 miles)
Total ascent	300m (985ft)
Time	5hr
Terrain	Canal-side path, minor roads, forest tracks and clear, firm paths.
Maps	OS Landranger 34, OS Explorer 400, Harvey Great Glen Way
Refreshments	The *Eagle* bar/restaurant at Laggan Locks.
Public Transport	Regular daily Scottish Citylink buses link Laggan with Inverness, Fort Augustus and Fort William. Schooldays-only Shiel Buses linking Gairlochy, Spean Bridge and Fort William, which will divert to Achnacarry on request to the driver.

Most of the day is spent on the northern shore of Loch Lochy, on forest tracks running parallel to the shore, and there is no exit from these until Clunes is reached. The slopes are often well wooded or forested, and timber harvesting and replanting ensures that over time, different places will feature different views. Detours from the Great Glen Way can be considered around Achnacarry, either to see St Ciaran's Church, tucked away in the woods, or to visit the Clan Cameron Museum. This is essentially Cameron country (or at least it became so after the Camerons concluded a 350-year feud against the MacIntoshes!).

Bear in mind that Gairlochy offers only a couple of B&Bs and a campsite off-route. During school termtime there are limited Shiel Buses linking Gairlochy with Spean Bridge and Fort William, but be sure to check their timetables carefully. Alternatively, ask in advance if your accommodation provider is able to offer pick-ups and drop-offs.

For 1:25K route map see booklet pages 10–17.

Cross the lock gates over the canal at **Laggan Locks**. Walk between cottages to pick up and follow a causeway road, crossing boggy ground beside **Cean Loch**. Pass some

View across Ceann Loch, which is part of Loch Lochy, towards the rugged slopes of Meall na Teanga

wooden lodges, then turn left at a road junction where the Invergarry Link joins from the right. Follow the road ahead until it crosses a bridge near **Kilfinnan Farm**. Turn right to follow a clear track uphill from the farm, enjoying views over the head of Loch Lochy. The gradient eases and the track keeps to the right as it passes the access for the Highland Lodges.

Go through a tall gate and continue straight ahead, reaching a junction of tracks near a communication mast, where a left turn is made down a forest track, almost exclusively flanked by birch. The track continues close to the shore of **Loch Lochy** and the trees are remarkably mixed, with conifers, alder and birch.

The level of **Loch Lochy** was raised 3.65m (12ft) during the construction of the Caledonian Canal. Its surface level is now 28.5m (94ft) above sea level, and its maximum depth is 40.5m (133ft). The loch is just short of 16km (10 miles) in length and only once exceeds 1.5km (1 mile) in width. It is said to be inhabited by a monster known as 'Lizzie', no doubt related to 'Nessie'.

153

Just off-route, beside the loch near the ruins of Glas-Dhoire, is a basic 'Trailblazer Rest' campsite. A key for the toilet needs to be obtained in advance via the Great Glen Way website or Caledonian Canal office.

Occasionally, the Great Glen Way Rangers station themselves at the Forest School and welcome the opportunity to have a chat with walkers.

Climb steeply uphill a short way from the shore and cross a bridge over the **Allt Glas-Dhoire**, walking among tall trees with no views, and pass a tall gateway. ◀ The track runs through younger forest where there is a margin of alder scrub, then another area of mature forest before crossing a bridge over the **Allt Glas-Dhoire Mór**. On the next gentle ascent and descent, clear-felling allows good views across the loch, but these are lost as the track climbs through more mature forest, passing another gateway before descending gently. The track rises uphill, then later passes a gateway and small waterfall on the Allt na Molaich. The track undulates past commercial conifers, as well as self-seeded alder and birch scrub, along with bracken, brambles and tufts of heather.

The track runs parallel to the shore of Loch Lochy until it swings right and goes through a tall gate to reach a car park. Continue past a couple of houses and wooden cabins, one of latter being the Clunes Forest School. ◀

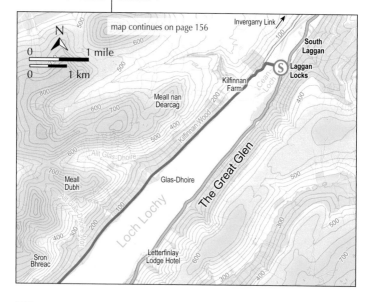

map continues on page 156

The Great Glen Way follows a long and easy forest track from Laggan to Bunarkaig

Turn left along the B8005 road at **Clunes**, passing modest forestry houses and a large white house. Continue along the road as the land near Loch Lochy is very wet and boggy, supporting profuse growths of bog myrtle. A fine variety of trees grace the shores of the loch, so that the area is rather like an arboretum. The most striking conifers are the giant redwoods, or sequoias, while the most impressive deciduous trees are the copper beeches. Continue along the road, crossing a bridge over the River Arkaig at **Bunarkaig**, where you reach a cluster of houses. ▸ Just up the road, another sign at a gateway invites visitors to make a detour to the **Clan Cameron Museum** at Achnacarry.

A short detour could be made to St Ciaran's Church, in a quiet woodland setting. Watch out for a sign showing the way along a track.

If you are a Cameron – and that includes members of nearly seventy 'sept' or sub-branch families! – then you should feel obliged to make a detour to the **Clan Cameron Museum**. The Museum, housed in a whitewashed 17th-century croft, is open each afternoon from April to early October, 1.30– 4.30pm, but 11am–5pm in July and August. There should be a notice by the gates on the B8005 road if the museum is open. There is an entrance charge (01397 712480, **www.clancameronmuseum.co.uk** and **www.clan-cameron.org**).

Follow the **B8005 road** until a left turn is waymarked down a clear gravel path, gradually descending across a slope of gnarled oaks, slender birch, beech and alder. The path wanders along the shore of Loch Lochy and crosses two footbridges as it rounds a small bay. Later, the path drifts away from the shore to cross a footbridge

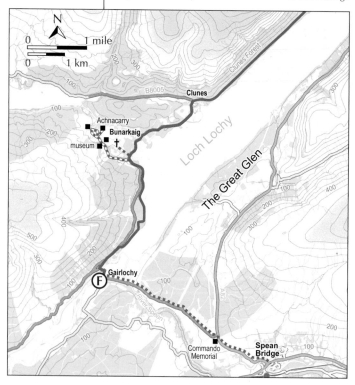

CLAN CAMERON

The Clan Cameron has a long association with the Great Glen. Originally, there were three families – the McMartins of Letterfinlay, the McGillonies of Strone and the McSorlies of Glen Nevis. The first Chief of the combined families was Donald Dubh, born around 1400, and the most recent is Donald Angus Cameron of Locheil, the 27th Chief. Never shy of battle, the Camerons were described as 'fiercer than fierceness itself'. Their rallying cry was 'Sons of the hounds, come hither and get flesh!' The Camerons moved from Tor Castle to Achnacarry around 1660, and visitors will appreciate the attractions of the location, an easily defended mountain fastness with sheltered pasture.

The 19th Chief, the 'Gentle Locheil' supported Bonnie Prince Charlie in 1745, and in giving support, ensured that many other clans rallied to the cause. Despite early military success, the Prince's forces were soundly beaten at Culloden and Charles was lucky to escape with his life. In retribution for Locheil's support, the Duke of Cumberland destroyed the original timber-built Achnacarry House in 1746, and Locheil fled into exile. The current stone-built Achnacarry House dates from 1802, and the Clan Cameron has distinguished itself by raising generations of soldiery for the Queen's Own Cameron Highlanders. Achnacarry House was occupied by the military for most of the Second World War, when it was the Commando Basic Training Centre, featuring one of the most gruelling military training regimes in the world.

over the Allt Coire Choille-rais. Densely packed conifers allow little light to reach the ground, but birch trees fringe the loch shore. Later, the path passes fine beech trees, where bright green moss thrives, covering boulders and fallen tree trunks. Cross a footbridge and follow the path onwards, and look out for a prominent little lighthouse and signs that indicate where the **Caledonian Canal** leaves the loch. The path climbs steeply from the shore and reaches the B8005 road again.

Cross over and follow the path as it undulates across a forested slope, just above the road. The path joins the road just before a junction, where forking left leads down to a swing bridge over the Caledonian Canal at **Gairlochy**.

GAIRLOCHY

Gairlochy (Gaelic – *Gèarr Lòchaidh*) is 6km (4 miles) has won, or come runner-up, in the 'Waterway Length Competition' on several occasions. Note that Gairlochy isn't a village, but merely a scattering of houses, and if anything can't be obtained in the locality, then it is necessary to move far off-route.

Basic camping is permitted near the canal, but a key for the toilet at the canal lock must be obtained in advance via the Great Glen Way website or Caledonian Canal office. The Dalcomera B&B is the only lodging nearby, just a short walk along the B8004 road. This road also leads to the Gairlochy Holiday Park, which has a serviced campsite. Any further facilities are well off-route at Spean Bridge. Shiel Buses run a very limited schooldays-only service linking Gairlochy with Spean Bridge and Fort William. The nearest taxi service operates from Fort William.

SPEAN BRIDGE

Spean Bridge (Gaelic – *Drochaid Aonachain*) is 6km (4 miles) away from Gairlochy. The High Bridge, built by General Wade in 1736, was the first bridge to span the rocky gorge beside the village. The West Highland Railway, built to serve Fort William from 1889, was equipped with a station at Spean Bridge. Outside the village, at a junction with the Gairlochy road, is the celebrated Commando Memorial, dating from 1952.

There are a few accommodation options around Spean Bridge, including a hotel. There is a post office shop, with an ATM outside, as well as a restaurant. Regular daily Scottish Citylink bus services run to and from Fort William, Fort Augustus and Inverness. Stagecoach Highland buses run to and from Fort William, while schooldays-only Shiel Buses link Spean Bridge with Fort William and Gairlochy. Trains run to Fort William and Glasgow. Some accommodation providers in Spean Bridge offer lifts to and from Gairlochy, if given due notice.

INVERGARRY LINK

The Invergarry Link allows walkers to vary their journey along the Great Glen Way by passing through the village of Invergarry, instead of walking along the southern shore of Loch Oich. Invergarry offers slightly more in the way of lodgings and facilities than are found along the main route. However, using the link route shortens the distance from Fort Augustus on Stage 4 by 4km (2½ miles), while the distance to Gairlochy on Stage 5 is increased by 7.5km (4¾ miles). Overall, using the Invergarry Link means walking 3.5km (2¼ miles) more than the main Great Glen Way route, with 250m (820ft) of extra ascent.

STAGE 4A

Fort Augustus to Invergarry

Start	Tourist Information Centre, Fort Augustus (NH 378 094)
Finish	Invergarry (NH 307 011)
Distance	13.5km (8¼ miles)
Total ascent	190m (625ft)
Time	3hr 30min
Terrain	Minor roads, forest tracks and paths
Maps	OS Landranger 34, OS Explorer 400, Harvey Great Glen Way
Refreshments	Tea garden at Aberchalder Swing Bridge. Hotel/bar restaurant in Invergarry.
Public Transport	Regular daily Scottish Citylink buses link Invergarry with Fort William, Fort Augustus and Inverness.

After climbing beside a fine flight of locks to leave Fort Augustus, a level track runs beside the Caledonian Canal. Once the main road is reached at the Aberchalder Swing Bridge, it is worth making a detour to inspect the older, elegant Bridge of Oich. Afterwards, the Invergarry Link parts from the main Great Glen Way, to use forest paths and tracks. After climbing and traversing a forested slope, there is a short descent to Invergarry. Limited lodgings and bus services are available, while the Glengarry Heritage Centre lies off-route.

Follow route description for Stage 4 as far as the **Aberchalder Swing Bridge**. Use the safe pedestrian path across the bridge, then cross over the road to follow the pavement running parallel. By all means make a short diversion to study the **Bridge of Oich**, returning to the main road afterwards, and pass a small car park used by those visiting the bridge.

If you're interested in joining them, nip across the Aberchalder Swing Bridge to reach the **Bridge of Oich**. An older bridge was swept away in devastating floods during 1849, when the embankment of the Caledonian Canal was also breached. Five years elapsed before a new bridge was built, by a brewer-turned-engineer called James Dredge, from Bath. The Bridge of Oich looks like a slender suspension bridge, but was actually patented as a 'double cantilever', built on the 'taper principle'. The

map continues
from page 149

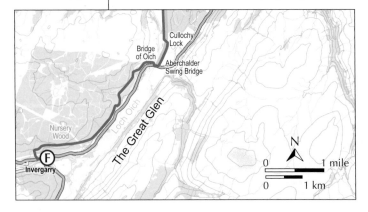

supporting chains gradually diminish as they spread outwards from the stout granite pillars that support them, and hold very little weight in the middle of the bridge. Apparently, if the bridge was ever severed in the middle, it would remain standing. The Bridge of Oich carried traffic up to 1932, but the busy A82 road now crosses a more solid-looking stone bridge nearby.

The interesting Bridge of Oich is easily visited by a short diversion off-route near Aberchalder.

A gravel path rises from the road and later makes a loop across a clear-felled slope. The path crosses a bridge, rises and falls, and follows a power line through a broad forest ride. When the path joins a track just above the main A82 road, turn right and follow the track, later rising to a junction. Keep left and there is a view down to the roof of the Invergarry Power Station. Keep following the track past **Nursery Wood**, and on a gentle downhill stretch, watch for a path off to the right. Follow it, and it later crosses back over the track.

The forest path running from Aberchalder towards Invergarry

A path drops downhill, passing conifers and rhododendron bushes, then tall oaks and rhododendron bushes, winding down to a telephone kiosk beside the A87 road at **Invergarry**. Turn left to pass a block of houses and the Invergarry Hotel to reach a junction with the main A82 road.

Invergarry (Gaelic – *Inbhir Garadh*) offers a small range of lodgings, including hotel, B&B and independent hostel. Regular daily Scottish Citylink buses link Invergarry with Fort William and Inverness. The Glengarry Heritage Centre is open from Easter to October, on Tuesday, Wednesday and Thursday, 11am–3pm, and can be visited free of charge (01809 501424/511278, **www.glengarryheritagecentre.com**).

STAGE 5A
Invergarry to Gairlochy

Start	Invergarry (NH 307 011)
Finish	Gairlochy Bottom Lock (NN 176 842)
Distance	26.5km (16½ miles)
Total ascent	400m (1310ft)
Time	6hr 30min
Terrain	Minor roads, forest tracks and paths
Maps	OS Landranger 34, OS Explorer 400, Harvey Great Glen Way
Refreshments	Shop at the Well of the Seven Heads.
Public Transport	Regular daily Scottish Citylink buses link Invergarry with Fort William, Fort Augustus and Inverness.

After leaving Invergarry by road, forest tracks lead uphill, gaining one good view of Loch Oich. A gradual descent leads to a road, where it is easy to detour off-route to the Well of the Seven Heads and a handy shop. An easy road walk takes the Invergarry Link to a road junction, where it re-joins the main Great Glen Way. The rest of the day is spent walking beside Loch Lochy.

The Invergarry Hotel overlooks the steep, wooded banks of the River Garry

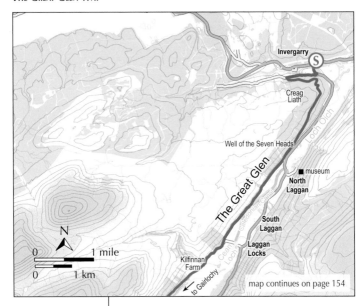

map continues on page 154

The Well of the Seven Heads Store and Well of the Seven Heads monument lies to the left, 600m further along the road. Take-away food is available.

To leave **Invergarry**, turn right along the main A82 road, and follow the pavement across a bridge over the River Garry. Turn right along a narrow road, passing a B&B, the Saddle Mountain Hostel and a couple of houses. Turn left up a forest track, which quickly swings left as it climbs. At a higher level, it swings right and passes a picnic table around 130m (425ft), where there is a view of **Loch Oich**. The track undulates gently, passes a couple of junctions and descends gently to return to the A82 road. ◄

The Well of the Seven Heads marks an historic and bloody act of retribution. On 25 September 1663, Alexander MacDonald, Chief of Keppoch, and his brother Ranald were killed by seven others during a clan dispute. While most of their kinsfolk seemed content to let the matter rest, Iain Lom, the Keppoch Bard, called for revenge, enlisting the support of MacDonald of Glengarry and Sir James MacDonald of Sleat. After two years, the seven culprits were tracked down to Inverlair, where they were slain and beheaded. The severed heads were washed in a well beside Loch Oich, then displayed at Invergarry Castle before being taken to Gallows Hill in Edinburgh on 7 December 1665. The Well of the Seven Heads is now enclosed in stone and bears a monument crowned with seven unhappy-looking heads, surmounted by a hand holding a dagger. The tale of murder and revenge is carved around all four sides in English, Gaelic, French and Latin.

Turn right and follow the path parallel to the road, later turning right again up a narrow minor road. This rises gently, undulates as it passes a few houses, then descends gently to a junction with another road. The Invergarry Link re-joins the main route of the Great Glen Way here.

Follow Stage 5 route description from here to Gairlochy.

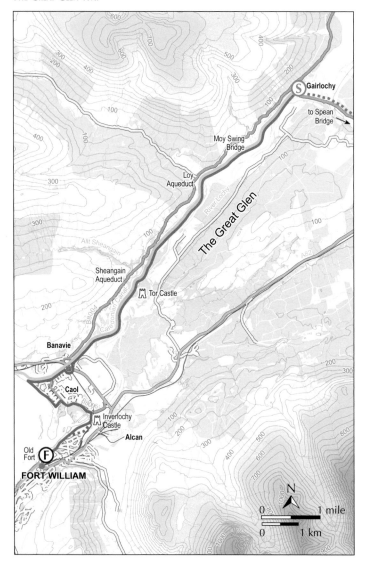

STAGE 6
Gairlochy to Fort William

Start	Gairlochy Bottom Lock (NN 176 842)
Finish	Railway station, Fort William (NN 105 742)
Distance	17km (10½ miles)
Total ascent	10m (35ft)
Time	4hr 30min
Terrain	Long, clear canal-side track, followed by low-level paths, tracks and roads near the coast.
Maps	OS Landranger 41, OS Explorers 392 and 400, Harvey Great Glen Way
Refreshments	Bar and restaurant at Banavie. Shops and bars at Corpach. Shops and take-aways at Caol. Plenty of bars, restaurants and cafés around Fort William.
Public Transport	Shiel Buses run a limited schooldays-only bus service linking Fort William, Gairlochy and Spean Bridge. Stagecoach buses link Banavie, Corpach and Caol with Fort William, and run most of the town services around Fort William. Trains between Fort William, Banavie and Corpach, as well as to Spean Bridge and Glasgow.

Most of this final stage is on a long and narrow 'island', flanked on one side by the Caledonian Canal and on the other by the River Lochy. This is an easy day's walk, descending in stages while following a clear canal-side track past locks. A series of roads and paths run close to the coast on the way to Fort William.

Facilities increase as the route progresses, and Fort William offers the largest concentration of lodgings and other services encountered since the start of the Great Glen Way in Inverness.

Leave **Gairlochy** and its swing bridge by following a track past Gairlochy Bottom Lock. The track drops a little, then crosses an overspill weir and enjoys a fine view of the broad and shingly River Lochy. Looking ahead you can

For 1:25K route map see booklet pages 6–10.

see Ben Nevis rising majestically from the further reaches of the Great Glen. Tall beech trees grace the canal-side, and later, on the far bank, a knoll bearing distinctive pine trees is an old burial ground. Also look across the canal to spot an inflowing stream, then reach the attractive **Moy Swing Bridge**.

> The **Moy Swing Bridge** simply allows the farmer from Moy to drive tractors and trailers down to his riverside meadows. Canal traffic, meanwhile, relies on a keeper to open and close the bridge on demand. However, the bridge is not mechanised, and only one half can be opened manually at a time; hence the need for a small boat so that the keeper can row across and open the other half. Basic camping, with no facilities, is permitted near the bridge.

Continue along the track; views across small meadows near the River Lochy are later closed off later as trees flank the canal-side. Further along, the canal crosses the **Loy Aqueduct** over the River Loy.

> To see the **Loy Aqueduct** properly turn sharp left on a downward track well after crossing over it, then retrace your steps afterwards. It is a splendid structure; the River Loy flows through a large central arch, while smaller arches on either side allow passage for man and beast.

The track later crosses an overspill, where excess water flows down into the River Lochy. Look across the canal to see a knoll crowned with a few pine trees, which is another old burial ground. The track rises then falls gently, passing abundant birch trees on the little hill of Druim na h-Atha, then a cottage. Continue enjoying the variety of trees alongside, and look across the water to spot a stream feeding water into the canal.

It is quite possible to cross the **Sheangain Aqueduct** without noticing, but take a few minutes to have a proper look at it.

Use a narrow path to descend from the embankment to gain a view of the three arched tunnels. Two carry water from the **Allt Sheangain**, while the third covers a stone-paved passage for man and his animals.

Not far from the Sheangain Aqueduct, **Tor Castle** overlooks the River Lochy. It was built by the MacIntoshes, who vacated it towards the end of the 13th century. Some time later it was occupied by the Camerons, sparking a feud between the two clans that spanned some 350 years, continuing even after the Camerons abandoned the property in 1660 and went to settle in Achnacarry. There is a B&B near the castle.

The canal curves gently left and right and for brief periods there are no signs of habitation, while a splendid variety of trees flank both banks; follow the track onwards, passing through a gate beside tall pines. Banavie Top Jetty is reached. Walk downhill in stages alongside the celebrated stepped locks known as Neptune's Staircase to reach the busy A830 at Banavie Swing Bridge.

Walkers on the clear canal-side track between Gairlochy and Banavie are passed by a cruiser

The lock at the top of Neptune's Staircase

Neptune's Staircase is an inspired name for the tightly packed series of eight canal locks at Banavie. The arrangement is difficult to see in its entirety, and the best views are those seen in the aerial shots used for postcards. Canal cruisers can pass from top to bottom in about ninety minutes, including the road and rail swing bridges at the bottom, but the time taken can almost double if craft pass through in the other direction at the same time.

Banavie (Gaelic – *Banbhaidh*) is a little village with only a few facilities. The Moorings Hotel, a couple of guest houses and a hostel are available, along with a canal-side gift shop that also offers teas. Basic camping is available beside the canal. There are regular daily bus and train services to and from Corpach and Fort William, as well as a schooldays-only service back to Gairlochy.

Cross the busy A830 road with care and turn left to pass **Banavie Station**. Turn right at a junction, over a level crossing, and continue along the road almost as far as a little pub restaurant called Lochy. Head right up a path, as directed, to reach the Caledonian Canal again. Continue straight along the broad gravel track, flanked on the right by grassy, flowery waterside banks, with tall beech trees on the left often obscuring views of Caol. The canal describes a broad and graceful curve to the right, later passing an overspill, where excess water flows down into Loch Linnhe. When the Corpach Double Lock is reached, the Great Glen Way turns left down a path, but walkers might wish to continue to the nearby terminus of the **Caledonian Canal** at the Corpach Basin and explore the village of Corpach too.

CORPACH

Corpach (Gaelic – *A' Chorpaich*) is an interesting little village, well worth a visit, overlooking the western sea terminus of the Caledonian Canal. There is public access to the Corpach Sea Lock and Corpach Basin, where boats may be moored while they wait for a favourable tide. The Narrows nearby are dominated by a huge pulp and paper mill, which chews up trees from the surrounding forests. A popular attraction for those with an interest in geology is 'Treasures of the Earth', which focuses on mines, minerals, gemstones and fossils. Open daily, April to October 10am–5pm, July and August 9.30am–6pm. Limited opening in winter (01397 772283, www.treasuresoftheearth.co.uk). There is an entrance charge.

Corpach has a bunkhouse and a couple of independent hostels and B&B establishments. There is a post office inside the Co-op store, and an ATM outside. Toilets are available in the Kilmallie Hall, when open, while canal users have access to toilets and a basic camping pitch near the canal office. Another shop and a bar are also available, and there are regular daily bus and train services to and from neighbouring Banavie and Fort William.

Step down from the stout embankment of the **Caledonian Canal**, following a path across a footbridge below the overspill weir. Walk along a gravel coastal path hemmed in between the shore of Loch Linnhe and a sports pitch, to reach Erracht Drive, which is flanked by a broad coastal green, in the village of **Caol**.

Caol (Gaelic – *Caol Loch Abar*) is a village close to The Narrows, where Loch Linnhe turns a right-angle corner and becomes known as Loch Eil. There are a couple of shops, pubs and take-aways, a post office, toilets and regular daily bus services to and from neighbouring Fort William, Corpach and Banavie.

INVERLOCHY CASTLE

The Comyns were a powerful Scottish family with two branches, the Red Comyns and the Black Comyns. The Red Comyns built Inverlochy Castle (*Gaelic* – Inbhir Lòchaidh) in 1280 and surrounded it with a moat connected to the River Lochy. The four-square thick stone walls are protected by drum towers at each corner, the largest being Comyn's Tower. There was probably a timber-built Great Hall inside the walls. The castle is always open and there is no entrance charge.

The Red Comyns and Black Comyns supported John Balliol's claim to the Scottish throne, and therefore attracted the enmity of Robert the Bruce. The MacDonalds supported Bruce, and in 1297 their vessels engaged Comyn vessels off Inverlochy, resulting in the sinking of two ships. The Comyns were later defeated in battle at Inverurie in May 1308, and Bruce granted Inverlochy Castle to the MacDonalds.

In the 15th century the MacDonalds were often in conflict with the Stuarts, who sat on the Scottish throne. Following a MacDonald raid on Inverness, James I sent a force commanded by the Earl of Mar to Inverlochy in 1431. As the army camped by the river they were picked off by MacDonald bowmen from the strategic hill of Tom na Faire, losing a thousand men. In 1645 there was another battle, this time between the Royalist army of Charles I, led by the Marquis of Montrose (with MacDonald support), and a Covenanting force led by the Marquis of Argyll (with Campbell support). Again, the strategic hill of Tom na Faire was put to good use by the Royalists; despite their smaller force they suffered only 20 casualties, while their opponents suffered 1500.

Following the construction of a fort at Fort William in the late 17th century (see below), Inverlochy Castle fell from favour. Military might was further consolidated when General Wade built a road from Fort William to Fort Augustus, passing Inverlochy Castle and completed in 1727. The castle was abandoned and was used by the Invergarry Ironworks from 1729 to 1736 as a store for pig iron.

Continue along Erracht Drive, turning left at the end along Glenmallie Road. Turn right at a bus stop to follow the **B8006**, Kilwallie Road, passing a B&B and a primary school on the way out of the village. The road runs parallel to the **River Lochy**. When it rises onto a railway bridge, turn right to cross the Soldier's Bridge, a long wooden footbridge mounted on top of a pipe, running parallel to the railway bridge over the river. Stepping down from the bridge, consider making a detour beneath the railway line to visit the nearby **Inverlochy Castle**.

Cross a bridge over the tailrace stream flowing from the **Alcan** aluminium works. ▶ Turn right to pick up and follow a path into a field, drifting left away from a narrow footbridge over the tailrace. The flow of the water is so strong here that the little footbridge vibrates! Follow the riverside path past a sports pitch, then go through a kissing gate and continue across a rushy meadow. Enter woodland and follow the path across a couple of small footbridges. Alder trees tend to screen both the river and the Inverlochy suburbs of Fort William from sight. Turn

At peak high tides, there is an alternative route straight ahead through the suburbs.

A pleasant green space just off the High Street in Fort William

left, then right to cross a bridge over the River Nevis. Ben Nevis rises far inland to the left, while the waters of Loch Linnhe are nearby.

Briefly follow a brick-paved road past a few houses, then follow a clear path alongside a 'shinty' pitch (shinty is a popular Gaelic sport that resembles hockey). The path reaches a busy roundabout beside McDonald's restaurant in Fort William. Keep right to walk round the roundabout and reach the ruins of the **Old Fort**, where a few low walls stand above the shore of Loch Linnhe. A stone monument marks the end of the Great Glen Way.

> The original '**Old Fort**' was a timber structure, built by General Monck to house 250 men. He referred to it as 'the fort of Inverlochy' in 1654, when writing to advise Oliver Cromwell of its completion. A stone fort was constructed in 1690 by General Mackay, housing 1000 men and defended by 15 guns. It was named in honour of King William, a member of the Dutch House of Orange, who fought a decisive battle against King James in that year. William ruled Britain jointly with his wife, Mary, the daughter of James II of Scotland. General Gordon attacked the fort during the 1715 rebellion, then in 1746 Sir Ewen Cameron attacked it. The fort was largely dismantled and the land bought by the West Highland Railway Company in 1889. They pushed a railway through the site, leaving only the small portion of the original walls seen today, which includes a sally port. The original stone-arched gateway to the fort was rebuilt and now serves as the entrance to a small graveyard off the busy Belford Road in Fort William.

To walk from the Old Fort into town, the best way is to double back to McDonald's restaurant, then cross a road and walk across Morrison's supermarket car park to reach the railway station or bus station. There is immediate access to the centre of **Fort William** by way of an underpass (see 'First/Last Night: Fort William' in the Introduction).

APPENDIX A
Useful information

Great Glen Way
Great Glen Way Rangers
Auchterawe
Fort Augustus
Inverness-shire PH32 4BT
tel 01320 366633
greatglenway@highland.gov.uk

Great Glen Way official website
www.outdoorhighlands.co.uk/long-distance-trails/great-glen-way-2
Note that the former (and easier)
www.greatglenway.com
still redirects to the above address.

Scottish Outdoor Access Code
www.outdooraccess-scotland.com

Caledonian Canal
Caledonian Canal Office
Seaport Marina
Muirtown Wharf
Inverness IV3 5LE
tel 01463 233140

Caledonian Canal Visitor Centre
Fort Augustus
tel 01320 366493
www.scottishcanals.co.uk/our-canals/caledonian-canal

Public Transport
Traveline Scotland
tel 0871 200 2233
www.travelinescotland.com
Up-to-date information about trains, buses or ferries (smartphone app available).

Inverness Airport
tel 01667 462445
www.hial.co.uk/inverness-airport

Cross Country Trains
www.crosscountrytrains.co.uk

Virgin Trains
www.virgintrains.co.uk

East Coast
www.eastcoast.co.uk

First ScotRail
www.scotrail.co.uk

Eurolines
www.eurolines.com

National Express
www.nationalexpress.com

Scottish Citylink
www.citylink.co.uk

Stagecoach
www.stagecoachbus.com

Caledonian Discovery Cruises
www.caledonian-discovery.co.uk

Cruise Loch Ness
www.cruiselochness.com

Accommodation
The Great Glen Way Accommodation and Services Guide contains an up-to-date list of accommodation options, as well as notes about a wealth of services along the course of the Great Glen Way. The guide is available from tourist information centres, or as a free download from the Great Glen Way website.

Visit Scotland
tel 0845 8591006 (from UK) or
tel +44 (0)131 5242121 (from abroad)
www.visitscotland.com

Scottish Youth Hostels Association
www.syha.org.uk

Baggage Transfer
Great Glen Way Baggage Shuttle and Support
West Lewiston
Drumnadrochit IV63 6UW
tel 01456 450550
mob 07711 429616
www.lochnesstravel.com

Great Glen Baggage Transfer
The Old Post Office
Invermoriston IV63 7YA
tel 01320 351322
mob 07920 745172
www.greatglenwaybaggagetransfer.co.uk

Tourist Information Centres
Fort William
TIC, 15 High Street
Fort William PH33 6DH
tel 0845 2255121
email via www.visitscotland.com

Invergarry
Glengarry Heritage Centre
Invergarry PH35 4HG
tel 01809 501424
centre@glengarryheritagecentre.com

Fort Augustus
TIC, Car Park
Fort Augustus PH32 4DD
tel 01320 366779
email via www.visitscotland.com

Drumnadrochit
TIC, Car Park
Drumnadrochit IV63 6TX
tel 01456 459086
email via www.visitscotland.com

Inverness
TIC, Castle Wynd
Inverness IV2 3BJ
tel 01463 252401
email via www.visitscotland.com

Tourist Attractions
West Highland Museum
Fort William
tel 01397 702169
www.westhighlandmuseum.org.uk

Treasures of the Earth
Corpach
tel 01397 772283
www.treasuresoftheearth.co.uk

Clan Cameron Museum
Achnacarry
tel 01397 712090
www.clancameronmuseum.co.uk

Highland and Rare Breeds Park
Fort Augustus
tel 01320 366433

Urquhart Castle
Drumnadrochit
tel 01456 450551

Nessieland
Drumnadrochit
tel 01456 450342

Loch Ness Exhibition Centre
Drumnadrochit
tel 01456 450573

Inverness Museum and Art Gallery
Inverness
tel 01463 234353

Emergency Services
For police, ambulance, fire, mountain rescue
or coastguard, dial 999 or 112.

APPENDIX B
Accommodation along the route

Accommodation is listed roughly in the order it appears to a walker heading south to north, from Fort William to Inverness (walkers heading north to south should read the list in reverse). Hotels, guest houses, B&Bs, hostels, bunkhouses and campsites are included; self-catering is not, but such accommodation could be used as a base, so long as it was near the frequent bus services that operate through the Great Glen. Take particular note of addresses that lie off-route. Generally speaking, anything more than 1km (½ mile) from the Great Glen Way is off-route. Only sample addresses are given for Fort William and Inverness, as there is plenty of choice available. It's probably more important for walkers to know about solitary addresses in more remote areas.

Fort William

There is plenty of accommodation in Fort William, and this is just a central selection. For more addresses contact the Visitor Information Centre, tel 01397 701801.

Premier Inn
Loch Iall An Aird
Fort William PH33 6AN
tel 0871 5278402

Best Western Imperial Hotel
Fraser Square
Fort William PH33 6DW
tel 0844 3876092

The Alexandra Hotel
The Parade
Fort William PH33 6AZ
tel 01397 702241

Berkeley House
Belford Road
Fort William PH33 6BT
tel 01397 701185

Ben View Guest House
Belford Road
Fort William PH33 6ER
tel 01397 702966

Craig Nevis Guest House
Belford Road
Fort William PH33 6BU
tel 01397 702023

Fort William Backpackers
Alma Road
Fort William PH33 6HB
tel 01397 700711

Guisachan House B&B
Alma Road
Fort William PH33 6HA
tel 01397 703797

Rhu Mhor Guest House
Alma Road
Fort William PH33 6BP
tel 01397 702213

Bank Street Lodge
Bank Street
Fort William PH33 6AY
tel 01397 700070
mob 07979 432105

6 Caberfeidh B&B
Fassifern Road
Fort William PH33 6BE
tel 01397 703756

Constantia House B&B
Fassifern Road
Fort William PH33 6BD
tel 01397 702893

Stobahn Guest House
Fassifern Road
Fort William PH33 6BD
tel 01397 702790

Glen Nevis (off-route)

Ben Nevis Guest House
Nevis Bridge
Glen Nevis
Fort William PH33 6PF
tel 01397 708817

Glen Nevis Youth Hostel
Glen Nevis
Fort William PH33 6SY
tel 01397 702336

Glen Nevis Campsite
Glen Nevis
Fort William PH33 6SX
tel 01397 702191

Lochyside

Lochan Cottage Guest House
Lochyside PH33 7NX
tel 01397 702695

Corpach

Blacksmith's Hostel & Smiddy Bunkhouse
Station Road
Corpach PH33 7JH
tel 01397 772467

Farr Cottage Lodge Hostel
Corpach PH33 7LR
tel 01397 772315

The Neuk B&B
Corpach PH33 7LR
tel 01397 772244

Mansefield House B&B
Corpach PH33 7LT
tel 01397 772262

Glenafton B&B
Albyn Drive
Corpach PH33 7LW
tel 01397 773191
mob 07884 314401

Banavie
The Moorings Hotel
Banavie PH33 7LY
tel 01397 772797

Chase the Wild Goose Hostel
Banavie PH33 7LZ
tel 01397 772531

Glenshian Guest House
Banavie PH33 7LY
tel 01397 772174

Carinbrook Guest House
Banavie PH33 7LX
tel 01397 772318

Treetops B&B
Badabrie
Banavie PH33 7LX
tel 01397 772496

Braeburn B&B
Badabrie
Banavie PH33 7LX
tel 01397 772047

Tor Castle
Torcastle House
Torcastle
Banavie PH33 7PB
tel 01397 701633

Moy Bridge
Very basic campsite with no
facilities.

Gairlochy
Basic campsite at Gairlochy
Locks.

Dalcomera B&B
Gairlochy PH34 4EQ
tel 01397 712778
mob 07752 892561

Dreamweavers B&B
Earendil
Mucomir PH34 4EQ
tel 01397 712548

Gairlochy Holiday Park
Campsite
Gairlochy Road PH34 4EQ
tel 01397 712711

Spean Bridge (off-route)
Old Pines Hotel
Gairlochy Road
Spean Bridge PH34 4EG
tel 01397 712324

Coinachan Guest House
Gairlochy Road
Spean Bridge PH34 4EG
tel 01397 712417

Aonach Mor Hotel
Spean Bridge PH34 4DX
tel 01397 712351

Inverour Guest House
Spean Bridge PH34 4EU
tel 01397 712218

Smiddy House Guest House
Spean Bridge PH34 4EU
tel 01397 712335

Milton Spean Bridge Hotel
Spean Bridge PH34 4ES
tel 01397 712250

Glas-Dhoire
Very basic 'Trailblazer Rest'
campsite.

South Laggan
Basic campsite at Laggan
Locks.

Forest Lodge Guest House
South Laggan PH34 4EA
tel 01809 501219

Great Glen Hostel
South Laggan PH34 4EA
tel 01809 501430

Bonnie Lilac Cottage B&B
South Laggan PH34 4EA
tel 01809 501410

North Laggan
Great Glen Water Park
North Laggan PH34 4EA
tel 01809 501381

Ban-Draiodh B&B
North Laggan PH34 4EB
tel 01809 501280
mob 07789 415568

Leitirfearn
Very basic 'Trailblazer Rest'
campsite.

Invergarry
Saddle Mountain Hostel
Mandally Road,
Invergarry PH35 4HP
tel 01809 501412

Invergarry Hotel
Invergarry PH35 4HJ
tel 01809 501206

Glengarry Castle Hotel
Invergarry PH35 4HW
tel 01809 501254

Nursery Cottages
Invergarry PH35 4HL
tel 01809 501297

Glen Albyn Lodge B&B
Invergarry PH35 4HL
tel 01809 501348

Glengarry (off-route beyond Heritage Centre)
Craigard Guest House
Invergarry PH35 4HG
tel 01809 501258

Ardgarry Farm B&B
Invergarry PH35 4HG
tel 01809 501226

Faichemard Farm Campsite
Invergarry PH35 4HG
tel 01809 501314

Aberchalder Swing Bridge
Basic campsite with no facilities.

Aberchalder (off-route)
Netherwood B&B
Newtown
Aberchalder PH35 4HT
tel 01320 366550

Kytra Lock
Very basic 'Trailblazer Rest' campsite.

Fort Augustus
Tigh na Mairi B&B
Canalside
Fort Augustus PH32 4BA
tel 01320 366766

The Holt B&B
Canalside
Fort Augustus PH32 4BA
tel 01320 366202

Bank House B&B
Station Road
Fort Augustus PH32 4AY
tel 01320 366755

Caledonian House B&B
Station Road
Fort Augustus PH32 4AY
tel 01320 366236
mob 07967 589120

Caledonian Cottage B&B
Station Road
Fort Augustus PH32 4AY
tel 01320 366305

Kings Inn B&B
Station Road
Fort Augustus PH32 4AY
tel 01320 366406

Abbey Cottage B&B
Fort Augustus PH32 4BD
tel 01320 310524

Richmond House Hotel
Fort Augustus PH32 4BD
tel 01320 366719

Caledonian Hotel
Fort Augustus PH32 4BQ
tel 01320 366256

Oaklands B&B
Fort William Road
Fort Augustus PH32 4BQ
tel 01320 366487

Cumberland's Campsite
Fort Augustus PH32 4BG
tel 01320 366257

Stravaigers Lodge Hostel
Fort Augustus PH32 4BG
tel 01320 366257

Sonas B&B
Fort Augustus PH32 4DH
tel 01320 366291

Morag's Lodge Hostel
Bunoich Brae
Fort Augustus PH32 4DG
tel 01320 366289

Rose Cottage B&B
Fort Augustus PH32 4BN
tel 01320 366639
mob 07729 311488

Thistle Dubh B&B
Fort Augustus PH32 4BN
tel 01320 366380
mob 07966 944109

Three Bridges B&B
Fort Augustus PH32 4BN
tel 01320 366712

The Inch Hotel
Fort Augustus PH32 4BL
tel 01456 450900

Inver Coille (from low-level route only)
Inver Coille Campsite
Invermoriston IV63 7YE
tel 01320 351224

Invermoriston
Fern Cottage B&B
Dalcataig
Invermoriston IV63 7YG
tel 01320 351262

Lann Dearg Studios B&B
Dalcataig
Invermoriston IV63 7YG
tel 01320 351353

Glenmoriston Arms Hotel
Invermoriston IV63 7YA
tel 01320 351206

Bracarina House B&B
Invermoriston IV63 7YA
tel 01320 351279
mob 07548 819020

Darroch View B&B
Invermoriston IV63 7YA
tel 01320 351388
mob 07880 982066

Bracadale B&B
Skye Road
Invermoriston IV63 7YA
tel 01320 351258
mob 07516 724168

Craik na Dav
Invermoriston IV63 7YA
tel 01320 351277
mob 07905 449691

**Alltsigh
(low-level route only)**
Briarbank B&B
Alltsigh
Invermoriston IV63 7YD
tel 01320 351381

Loch Ness Youth Hostel
Alltsigh
Invermoriston IV63 7YD
tel 01320 351274

Clunebeg
Clunebeg Lodge B&B
Drumnadrochit IV63 6US
tel 01456 459087

Borlum (off-route)
Caravan and Camping Park
Borlum Farm
Drumnadrochit IV63 6XN
tel 01456 450220

Lewiston
Loch Ness Inn
Lewiston IV63 6UW
tel 01456 450991

Glen Rowan Guest House
Lewiston IV63 6UW
tel 01456 450232

Loch Ness Backpackers
Lodge
East Lewiston IV63 6UJ
tel 01456 450807

Aislach B&B
East Lewiston IV63 6UJ
tel 01456 459466

Woodlands Guest House
East Lewiston IV63 6UJ
tel 01456 450356

Kilmore Farmhouse B&B
Kilmore IV63 6UF
tel 01456 450524

Benleva Hotel
Kilmore IV63 6UH
tel 01456 450080

Drumnadrochit
The Glen B&B
Village Green
Drumnadrochit IV63 6TX
tel 01456 450279

Fiddlers Rest B&B
Village Green
Drumnadrochit IV63 6TX
tel 01456 450678

Morlea B&B
Village Green
Drumnadrochit IV63 6TX
tel 01456 450410

Greenlea B&B
Village Green
Drumnadrochit IV63 6TX
tel 01456 450546

Bridgend House B&B
Village Green
Drumnadrochit IV63 6TX
tel 01456 450865

Drumnadrochit Hotel
Drumnadrochit IV63 6TU
tel 01456 450218

Loch Ness Lodge Hotel
Drumnadrochit IV63 6TU
tel 01456 450342

Springburn B&B
Cannich Road
Drumnadrochit IV63 6TZ
tel 01456 450856

Glenkirk B&B
Drumnadrochit IV63 6TZ
tel 01456 450802

Kilmichael House B&B
Drumnadrochit IV63 6TZ
tel 01456 450703

Abriachan
Camping Pod Heaven
Angelshare
Abriachan IV3 8LB (off-route)
mob 07810 187162

Eco-Campsite and basic trail
cabin
Abriachan IV3 8LB
tel 01463 861462

Inverness
There is plenty of accommodation in Inverness, and this
is just a central selection. For
more addresses, contact the
Tourist Information Centre,
tel 01463 252401.

Premier Inn
Glenurquhart Road
Inverness IV3 5TD
tel 0845 5279938

Hebrides Guest House
Glenurquhart Road
Inverness IV3 5TD
tel 01463 220062

Bught Caravan Park &
Campsite
Bught Lane
Inverness IV3 5SR
tel 01463 236920.

Cavell House B&B
Island Bank Road
Inverness IV2 4SX
tel 01463 232850

River View Guest House
Island Bank Road
Inverness IV2 4SX
tel 01463 235557

Moray Park Guest House
Island Bank Road
Inverness IV2 4SX
tel 01463 233528

Talisker B&B
Ness Bank
Inverness IV2 4SF
tel 01463 236221

Macrae House
Ness Bank
Inverness IV2 4SF
tel 01463 243658

The Glenmoriston Town
House Hotel
Ness Bank
Inverness IV2 4SF
tel 01463 223777

The Waterside Hotel
Ness Bank
Inverness IV2 4SF
tel 01463 233065

The Alexander Guest House
Ness Bank
Inverness IV2 4SF
tel 01463 231151

Glen Mhor Hotel
Ness Bank
Inverness IV2 4SF
tel 01463 234308

Ness Bank Guest House
Ness Bank
Inverness IV2 4SF
tel 01463 232939

Outside Inverness Castle, Flora MacDonald gazes towards the Great Glen

Wychway B&B
Haugh Road
Inverness IV2 4SD
tel 01463 239299

Castle View Guest House
Ness Walk
Inverness IV3 5NE
tel 01463 241443

Inverness Student Hotel
Culduthel Road
Inverness IV2 4AB
tel 01463 236556

Royal Highland Hotel
Station Square
Inverness IV1 1LG
tel 01463 231926

MacDougall Clansman Hotel
Church Street
Inverness IV1 1ES
tel 01463 713702

Youth Hostel
Victoria Drive
Inverness IV2 3QB
tel 01463 231771

APPENDIX C

Timeline history

The following timeline history is biased in favour of events that took place in the Great Glen and the Highlands of Scotland, at the expense of events that took place around Edinburgh or the Scots/English border.

7500BC	Mesolithic hunter-gatherers made their way along the Highland coast, carrying simple stone tools and pots. They left little trace of their passing, except where they settled long enough to create 'middens' (rubbish dumps of bones and shell fragments).
3000BC	Neolithic migration through Scotland, with the construction of chambered cairns. The 'Fortingall Yew' sprouted around this time and probably remains the oldest living tree in Europe.
300BC	During the Iron Age, Celtic tribes from southern Scotland and Ireland migrated northwards, building forts (dun) and stone towers (brochs).
AD43	Emissaries were sent from the Orkney Islands to make contact with Claudius during the Roman conquest of Britain. A tribe living in the Great Glen was named the Caledones at this time; the name was later used to describe almost all the tribes living in the Highlands of Scotland.
AD84	The battle of Mons Graupius, thought to be in the Grampian, or Moray, region. Agricola led four legions of Roman soldiers into battle against the native Caledonii, who were led by Calgacus. Although the Romans won the battle, they were never able to subdue the Highlands, and withdrew southwards. The Romans were impressed by the hardy nature of the tribes, while Tacitus said they had red hair and large limbs.
AD122	Hadrian's Wall was constructed across northern England.
AD142	The Antonine Wall was constructed across central Scotland.
AD250	The 'Scots', who were an Irish tribe, began to conduct raids along the western seaboard of Scotland.
AD297	A Roman writer, Eumenius, was the first to mention the Picts by name, although it is thought they were already well established in the land.
AD367	The Scots, Saxons and Franks came into greater contact with the Picts as they worked their way into Scotland.
AD392	St Ninian introduced Christianity to the far south of Scotland at Whithorn.
AD400–500	The legendary Pictish warrior Cruithne was said to have ruled over much of Scotland for 100 years. On his death, each of his seven sons ruled over part of his kingdom. Around AD500, the Western Highlands were already under Scots control, while Fergus established the kingdom of Dalriada, based around Argyll and the islands. The Picts found themselves pushed more to the north and east of Scotland.
AD563	St Columba was exiled from Ireland and settled on Iona.

AD565	St Columba travelled through the Great Glen and is credited with seeing the Loch Ness 'monster' on his way to Inverness. He met the Pictish king Brude and duelled with his magician Briochan. Around this time, there were essentially four distinct civilisations in Scotland: the northern Picts and southern kinsmen; the Scots of Dalriada; the Britons in central Scotland, with the Saxons and Angles further south. This situation led to a period of conflict and strife. Cumin, a follower of Columba, established a monastic settlement in the middle of the Great Glen.
AD603	King Aedan of Dalriada united the Scots and Picts in an attempt to drive the Angles southwards into Northumbria. He was defeated in battle.
AD657–85	Bridei, a Pictish ruler, attacked the Argyll capital of the Scots and subdued them, and later launched an assault against the expanding Northumbrian kingdom, leading to a short period of Pictish domination in Scotland.
AD706–24	The Pictish ruler Neachtan worried about religious authority and banished Christian monks from his kingdom. However, he later relented and joined a religious community.
AD731–61	Oengus Mac Fergus became the first king of both the Picts and the Scots, though he was unable to take the kingdom of Strathclyde. After his death, the Scots dissociated themselves from Pictish rule.
AD780	Invaders from Scandinavia appeared in small numbers.
AD789–820	A series of rulers, some Pictish and some Scots, ensured that the two kingdoms were basically unified throughout this period.
AD839	Increasing numbers of Norse invaders caused huge problems. The Picts and Scots united, but were defeated by the invaders, leaving the two kingdoms severed from each other.
AD842–48	Kenneth Mac Alpin, king of the Scots at Dalriada, moved to Scone and took with him the Lia Fáil, or Stone of Destiny, now known as the Stone of Scone. This ancient stone, reputedly carried by the Celts from Scythia to Ireland, and thence to Scotland, was always associated with the coronation of kings. With its aid, and much political and physical manoeuvring, Mac Alpin became the first true King of the Scots. The official language was Gaelic, as the Pictish language and culture quickly expired. However, Norse influence remained strong throughout the region.
AD850	Kenneth Mac Alpin conducted a series of raids on Northumbria.
AD900	Constantin II attempted to absorb Norse settlers into the emerging kingdom of Scotland.
1005–34	Malcolm II achieved Scottish unity and expelled the English.
1040	Duncan, heir of Malcolm, was killed by Macbeth, but not in the manner described by Shakespeare.
1057	Macbeth was killed by Malcolm III, who took the throne and instituted the royal House of Canmore.
1093	Death of St Margaret, founder of the modern city of Edinburgh, and wife of Malcolm III.
1124–53	David I introduced Norman culture to Scotland and built several abbeys in southern Scotland, including Jedburgh, Kelso, Melrose and Dryburgh.

1156	Somerled, progenitor of the great clans MacDonald and Ranald, led a force against the Norse and became ruler of old Dalriada, though the islands remained nominally under Norse control.
1263	The Norse relinquished control over the Hebrides after the Battle of Largs.
1280	Inverlochy Castle was built by the Comyns at the foot of Ben Nevis.
1290	The Scots queen Margaret, also known as the 'Maid of Norway', died on her way to marry Edward, son of Edward I of England. The Scots asked Edward I to decide who should rule Scotland out of a total of 13 claimants. Edward chose John Balliol, a man he could easily control.
1297–1305	William Wallace led a violent campaign against the English, and was eventually captured and executed.
1306–29	Robert the Bruce strove to gain the Scottish throne. During this campaign he was supported by the MacDonalds, and gave them Inverlochy Castle in 1308. After the defeat of Edward II at Bannockburn, the Treaty of Northampton recognised Scottish sovereignty.
1368	Edinburgh Castle was built.
1371–90	Robert II founded the royal House of Stewart. The king was often in conflict with the barons, as well as occasionally at war with the English.
1400	Birth of Donald Dubh, who became the first chief of the Clan Cameron, often in dispute with their Great Glen neighbours the MacIntoshes.
1431	The MacDonalds had raided Inverness, so James I sent a force commanded by the Earl or Mar to Inverlochy. The MacDonalds defeated them in the First Battle of Inverlochy
1472	Orkney and Shetland passed from Norse to Scottish control.
1488–1515	The Highlands received little interference during the reign of James IV, and the king was eventually killed in war against the English at Flodden.
1542	James V was defeated in battle by Henry VIII at Solway Moss.
1544	The Battle of the Shirts took place at Laggan in the Great Glen.
1560–87	A time of political and religious strife. In 1560 Mary, Queen of Scots, travelled from Catholic France to Calvinist Scotland and married Lord Darnley in 1565. He was murdered in 1567, and Mary married the Earl of Bothwell, resulting in her expulsion from Scotland. Imprisoned by her father's cousin Elizabeth I, Mary was executed in 1587.
1603	As Elizabeth I died without an heir, Mary's son, James VI of Scotland, was also crowned James I of England, although the Scottish and English parliaments remained separate. Political and religious strife continued.
1638–43	Both the Scottish and English parliaments rebelled against the rule of Charles I. The authority of Charles had already been challenged by the National Covenant in Scotland, and this led to Presbyterianism becoming the leading faith in Scotland. England descended into Civil War.

1645	During the Second Battle of Inverlochy, the Civil War gave long-standing rival clans a chance to settle differences. The Marquis of Montrose, with MacDonald support, fought on the Royalist side. A Covenanting force, led by the Marquis of Argyll with Campbell support, fought on the Parliamentarian side. The Royalists won, but retribution was swift and terrible.
1649–52	Following the execution of Charles I, Oliver Cromwell was made Lord Protector. He initiated a bloody campaign to clear the Scottish Highlands of Royalist support.
1654	A wooden fort was built by General Monck, and referred to as 'the fort of Inverlochy', following the abandonment of Inverlochy Castle nearby.
1660	The Restoration of the Monarchy. Charles II was invited back to England and the Covenanters were persecuted throughout Scotland. The Camerons abandoned Tor Castle and moved to Achnacarry.
1663–65	The 'Keppoch' murders, and the fierce retribution that resulted in the beheading of seven murderers at Inverlair, commemorated at the Well of the Seven Heads in the Great Glen.
1688–89	James VII of Scotland (and II of England) was ousted from the throne in favour of his daughter Mary, and her husband William of Orange. James's support-ers were known as 'Jacobites' and were defeated at the Battle of Killiecrankie. Presbyterianism was re-established in Scotland.
1690	General Mackay replaced 'the fort of Inverlochy' with a stone fort, which he named Fort William, in honour of the new king.
1692	Urquhart Castle was rendered unusable. Highlanders who refused to support the king were slaughtered at the infamous Massacre of Glencoe.
1707	The Scottish and English parliaments were united during the reign of Queen Anne.
1714	With the death of Queen Anne, George I, descended from a daughter of James VI of Scotland, was crowned king, inaugurating the Hanoverian succession.
1715	The First Jacobite Rebellion, following which a fort was established in the middle of the Great Glen.
1725	General Wade began constructing roads through the Highlands.
1726	The first plans for the Caledonian Canal through the Great Glen were drawn, but nothing was achieved on the ground.
1736	General Wade built the High Bridge over a gorge at Spean Bridge.
1745–1746	The Second Jacobite Rebellion, led by 'Bonnie Prince Charlie', who was a grandson of James VII of Scotland. Following initial surprising victories, his army of Highlanders pushed as far south as Derby. Charles would have pressed on to London, but for the counsel of his advisers. However, once he turned back towards Scotland, the Duke of Cumberland pursued the Scots to bloody defeat at Culloden, and wreaked havoc through the Great Glen. Charles was lucky to be able to escape with his life, aided at the end by Flora MacDonald. The fort in the middle of the Great Glen was rebuilt and named Fort Augustus after the 'Butcher' Duke of Cumberland.

1788	The death of 'Bonnie Prince Charlie' in Rome. (Interestingly, an early 19th-century monument raised in the Vatican in honour of the last of the Stuarts was partly funded by the Hanoverian King George IV.)
1790	The Forth and Clyde Canal was opened through central Scotland.
1800	The beginning of the brutal 'Highland Clearances' led to the massive depopulation of the Highlands, with much farmland turned over to sheep pasture. While some people moved elsewhere in Scotland, most were forced to emigrate to North America.
1803–22	The Caledonian Canal was cut through the Great Glen. Tourism in the area began to develop apace.
1837	Coronation of Queen Victoria.
1842–46	Railways finally linked London with Glasgow and Edinburgh. Fort William was lit using oil lamps.
1848	Queen Victoria purchased the Balmoral Estate in the Highlands.
1849	The Potato Famine hit the Highlands particularly hard, leading to one final clearance of the poorest part of the population from the land.
1854	The Bridge of Oich was constructed by James Dredge at Aberchalder.
1855	The Inverness and Nairn Railway was opened.
1864	The Creag Dunain Hospital opens near Inverness.
1876	The site of Fort Augustus was given to the Benedictines, who built an abbey there.
1883	A pony track was constructed from Glen Nevis to the summit of Ben Nevis.
1886	Foundation of the Scottish Home Rule Association.
1889	The West Highland Railway reaches Fort William.
1895	The development of a hydroelectric plant leads to electric lighting for Fort William.
1901	The death of Queen Victoria.
1903	The Invergarry and Fort Augustus Railway was opened, but was never extended through the Great Glen to Inverness as originally planned.
1928	The Foundation of the Scottish National Party.
1931	The British Aluminium (later Alcan) plant opened near Fort William, powered by an extensive hydroelectric scheme.
1934	First photograph of the Loch Ness 'monster' published, leading to an influx of visitors and the further development of the tourist trade.
1940–45	During the Second World War, Commandos were based at Achnacarry House, enduring one of the world's toughest training regimes.
1946	The Inverness and Fort Augustus Railway was closed.
1952	Queen Elizabeth, the Queen Mother, unveiled the Commando Memorial above Spean Bridge.
1953	Coronation of Queen Elizabeth II.

The Clan Cameron Museum is off-route at Achnacarry (Stage 2, S–N; Stage 5, N–S), but is worth a visit if you can spare the time

1964	The Forth Road Bridge was opened near Edinburgh. The Scottish Pulp and Paper Mill was opened near Fort William.
1970	The North Sea oil industry was developed, leading to increased prosperity in some parts of the Highlands.
1973	The United Kingdom joined the Common Market.
1979–2000	Scotland voted in two referenda on the issue of devolution, involving many years of debate, resulting in the election of a Scottish parliament.
2000	Inverness was granted a city charter.
2002	The Great Glen Way was officially opened by Prince Andrew, Earl of Inverness.
2003	The Land Reform (Scotland) Act came into force, clarifying and guaranteeing rights of access to the Scottish countryside.
2014	Work is completed on new high-level stretches of the Great Glen Way. A referendum posed the question 'Should Scotland be an independent country?', with 55.3 per cent of voters against and 44.7 per cent of voters for.
2015	In the General Election, an overwhelming number of Scottish National Party candidates were elected.

APPENDIX D
Gaelic–English glossary

The oldest place names in the Great Glen are Gaelic, since the language of the Picts has been lost. Gaelic thrives in the Highlands, and road signs throughout the region are often bilingual. Gaelic place names appear in abundance on maps, and they are often highly descriptive of landscape features.

Gaelic	English	Gaelic	English
abhainn	river	fionn	fair
allt	stream	gaoithe	wind
ard	high	garbh	rough
ath	ford	gearr	sharp
auch	field	glais	stream
bal/bally	township	glas/ghlas	grey
bàn/bhàn	white	gleann	glen/valley
bealach	pass/col	guala	shoulder
beag/bheag	small	inbhir	confluence
ben/beinn/bheinn	mountain	innis	island/field
breac/bhreac	speckled	iolaire	eagle
biorach	pointed	lagan	hollow
buidhe	yellow	leac	flat rock
caisteal	castle	leathan	broad
caol	narrow	loch	lake
caorach	rowanberry	lochan	small lake
carn	cairn	maol/mhaoile	bald
cioch/ciche	breast	meall	rounded hill
cir/chir	comb/crest	mhuileann	mill
clachan	farm/hamlet	monadh	mountain
cnoc	small hill	mór/mhór	big
coire/choire	corrie	mullach	summit
coille	wood	odhar	dappled
creag	crag	oighe	youth
dearg	red	reamhar	fat
donn	brown	righ	king
dubh	black	ruadh	russet
dun	fort	suidhe	seat
eas	waterfall	torr	small hill
eilean	island	uaine	green
fada/fhada	long	uisge	water

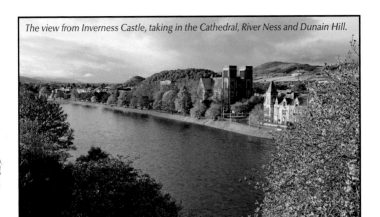
The view from Inverness Castle, taking in the Cathedral, River Ness and Dunain Hill.

DOWNLOAD THE ROUTE
IN GPX FORMAT

All the routes in this guide are available for download from:

www.cicerone.co.uk/801/GPX

as GPX files. You should be able to load them into most formats of mobile device, whether GPS or smartphone.

When you go to this link, you will be asked for your email address and where you purchased the guide, and have the option to subscribe to the Cicerone e-newsletter.

www.cicerone.co.uk

CICERONE GUIDES TO THE BRITISH ISLES

For full information on all our
guides, books and eBooks,
visit our website:
www.cicerone.co.uk.

Walking – Trekking – Mountaineering – Climbing – Cycling

Over 40 years, Cicerone have built up an outstanding collection of over 300 guides, inspiring all sorts of amazing adventures.

 Every guide comes from extensive exploration and research by our expert authors, all with a passion for their subjects. They are frequently praised, endorsed and used by clubs, instructors and outdoor organisations.

All our titles can now be bought as **e-books**, **ePubs** and **Kindle** files and we also have an online magazine – **Cicerone Extra** – with features to help cyclists, climbers, walkers and trekkers choose their next adventure, at home or abroad.

Our website shows any **new information** we've had in since a book was published. Please do let us know if you find anything has changed, so that we can publish the latest details. On our **website** you'll also find great ideas and lots of detailed information about what's inside every guide and you can buy **individual routes** from many of them online.

It's easy to keep in touch with what's going on at Cicerone by getting our monthly **free e-newsletter**, which is full of offers, competitions, up-to-date information and topical articles. You can subscribe on our home page and also follow us on **Facebook** and **Twitter** or dip into our **blog**.

Cicerone – the very best guides for exploring the world.

CICERONE

2 Police Square Milnthorpe Cumbria LA7 7PY
Tel: 015395 62069 info@cicerone.co.uk
www.cicerone.co.uk and **www.cicerone-extra.com**